Hacking Ma Bell
Youth International Party Line:
The First Three Years

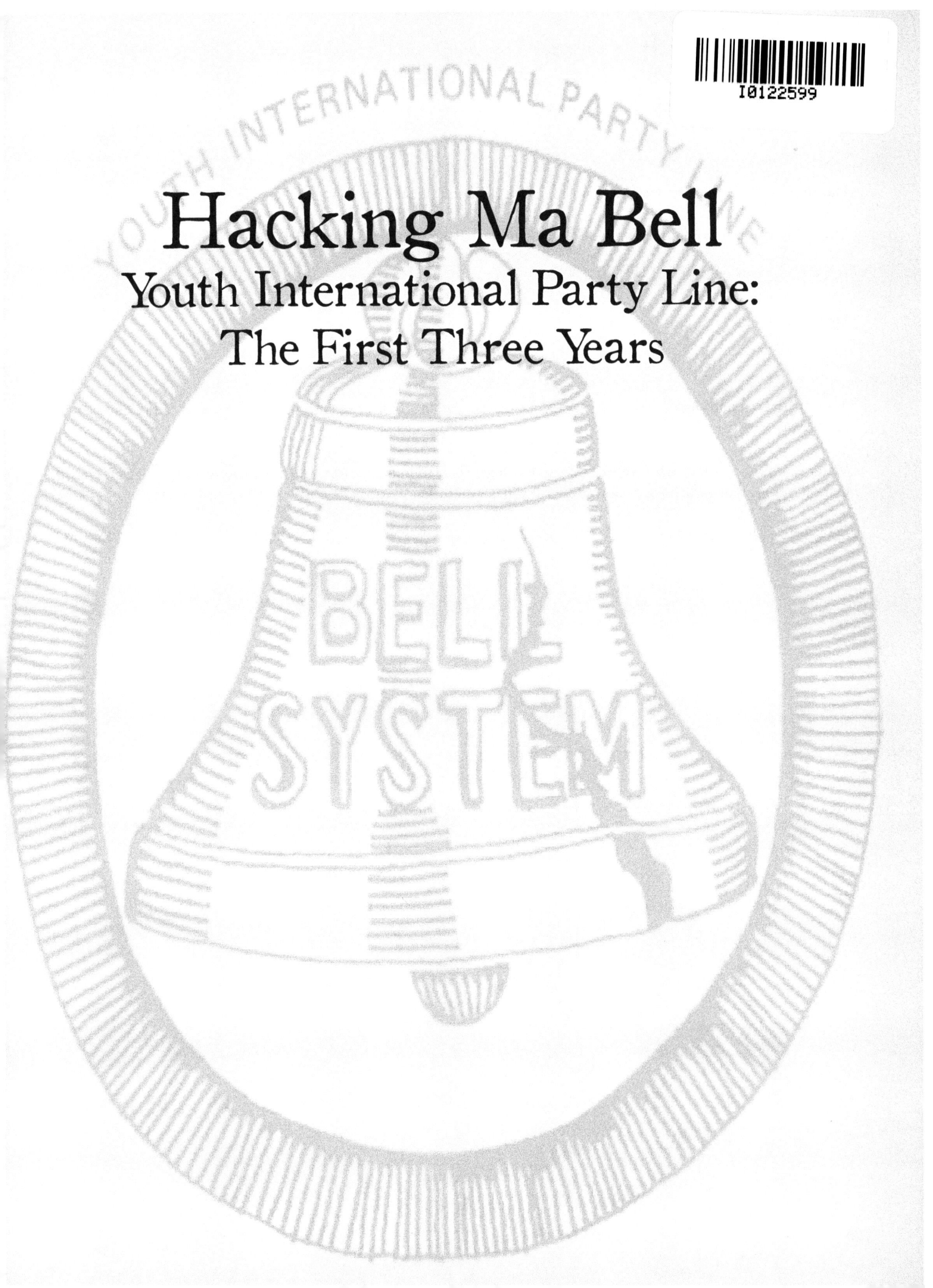

Hacking Ma Bell: The First Hacker Newsletter -Youth International Party Line, The First Three Years

This compilation first published in the United States in 2010 by Warcry Communications

ISBN 978-0-9842844-1-2

First Edition: June 2010

Warcry Communications was formed in 2010 to bring a voice to human, earth, and animal liberation struggles. For information, submission guidelines, bulk requests, or general inquiries, please contact:

info@voiceofthevoiceless.org

Hacking Ma Bell
Youth International Party Line:
The First Three Years

TAP was first published in June, 1971. The original purpose was to help the movement for change against the world's largest monopoly, The BELL TELEPHONE COMPANY. This was soon expanded to a fight against all corporations that were working AGAINST the people of the U.S. OUR purpose is to expose all the info we can get our hands on and let YOU be the judge of what to do with it.

TABLE OF CONTENTS

The Phone Phreak's Ten Commandments

I. Box thou not over thine home telephone wires, for those who doest must surely bring the full wrath of the Chief Special Agent down upon thy heads.

II. Speakest thou not of important matters over thine home telephone wires, for to do so is to risk thine right of freedom.

III. Use not thine own name when speaking to other Phreaks, for that every third Phreak is an FBI agent is well known.

IV. Let not overly many people know that thy be a Phreak, as to do so is to use thine own self as a sacrificial lamb.

V. If thou be in school, strive to get thine self good grades, for the Authorities well know that scholars never break the law.

VI. If thou workest, try to be a goodly employee, and impressest thine boss with thine enthusiasm, for important employees are often saved by their own bosses.

VII. Storest thou not thine stolen goodes in thine own home, for those who do are surely non-believers in the Bell System Security forces, and are not long for this world.

VIII. Attractest thou not the attention of the Authorities, as the less noticable thou art, the better.

IX. Makest sure thine friends are instant amnesiacs and will not remember that thou have called illegally, for their co-operation with the Authorities will surely lessen thine time of freedom on this Earth.

X. Supportest thou **TAP**, as it is thine newsletter, and without it, thy works will be far more limited.

INTRODUCTION

Youth International Party Line picked up where Steal This Book left off. Recognized as the first hacker newsletter, Y.I.P.L. (later Technological Assistance Party [T.A.P.]) offered readers visions of, and strategies for, a world free of charge. Since its beginnings as a tool to disseminate tactics to undermine AT&T's monopoly, to its evolution into a clearinghouse for scams to obtain free-everything. To some, Y.I.P.L. offered a blueprint for those wishing to live under the radar and above the law. Even more conservative elements could appreciate Y.I.P.L., those of a more pure-blood hacker ethos that emphasized the reverse-engineering of man-made systems over the fruits of circumvention. Either way, when the headline was "How To Not Get Caught Making Fake Credit Card Calls", Y.I.P.L. had everyone's attention.

A brief statement of purpose from its pages:

"TAP was first published in June, 1971. The original purpose was to help the movement for change against the world's largest monopoly, the Bell Telephone Company. This was soon expanded to a fight against all corporations that were working against the people of the U.S. OUR purpose is to expose all the info we can get our hands on and let YOU be he judge of what to do with it".

This collection is being offered to capture a crucial piece of hacker movement history, and timeless lessons from outlaw culture's most sophisticated - and intelligent - demographic. The obsolescence of the scams offered perhaps nullifies the demand for a legal disclaimer, but with articles titled "The Burglar's Tool Box", we'll probably print one anyway.

The history of Y.I.P.L. is largely offered in the newsletters themselves, but a few notes are in order: Y.I.P.L. was founded by Abbie Hoffman and Al Bell on, as legend has it, May Day, 1971. In the late-70's, "Tom Edison" took over the role as editor, and ran the publications for many years. After the firebombing of Edison's apartment in 1983, publication was passed to Cheshire Catalyst, who struggled to keep the publication alive until its peaceful death in 1984. Y.I.P.L. (then T.A.P.) enjoyed a brief resurrection in 1990.

What is offered here is a compilation of the first 3 years, issues 1 to 23. The youthful defiance and taunting of both the authorities and phone company make these issues a pleasure to read for anyone who appreciates an approach to change more direct than the ballot box - or just wants to cheer some Robin Hood-style outlaws from the sidelines.

For freedom from, and freedom to,
The Editors

A note on this collection: Compiling this material required drawing from some very old sources. A certain level of quality loss is inevitable when reprinting a 40-year-old publication. The text in parts can be illegibly small or faded. This material was taken from the highest quality sources available.

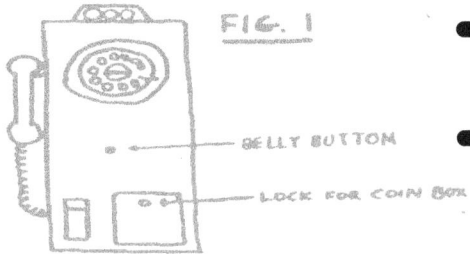

FIG. 1

BELLY BUTTON

LOCK FOR COIN BOX

FIG. 2

1971

GREEN

RED

YELLOW

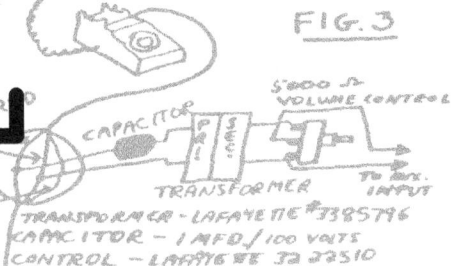

FIG. 3

CAPACITOR

5000 Ω
VOLUME CONTROL

TRANSFORMER

TO AMX.
INPUT

TRANSFORMER - LAFAYETTE #3385796
CAPACITOR - 1 MFD / 100 VOLTS
CONTROL - LAFAYETTE 32 22510

Published Monthly

THE YOUTH INTERNATIONAL PARTY LINE'S FIRST ISSUE

June, 1971

We at YIPL would like to offer thanks to all you phreeks out there. Most of you who are now receiving this met us in Washington on Mayday, where we distributed 10,000 promo flyers. So far we have received over 50 responses, complete with contributions, encouragement, and spirit. We may not have done well percentage-wise, but the fact that there are 50 people all over the country willing to fight back speaks for itself. We are sure that from the spirit of the response, YIPL membership will really skyrocket. However, more important than our numbers, in our opinion, is the feeling and motivation for this movement. The disappointment we feel toward Amerika has turned to hatred as we saw the futility of the movement to improve it, and to frustation as our outside efforts were repressed and forbidden. But we did not turn our backs on the movement for change. YIPL believes that education alone cannot affect the System, but education can be an invaluable tool for those willing to use it. Specifically, YIPL will show you why something must be done immediately in regard, of course, to the improper control of the communication in this country by none other than the BELL TELEPHONE COMPANY.

So if your friends want to get in on the fun, let them read your newsletter, and you might want to research your own questions in your local library, and help to start the education of your community of the phone company's part in the war against the poor, the non-white, the non-conformist, and in general, aginst the people. Show your neighbors, friends and the representatives of your area how the Bell System and the Amerikan government are co-conspirators. If your friends can't subscribe to YIPL, that; is cool, is convenient for our small staff, and is right on if they can send a buck as a donation and read your newsletter. We also need stamps, letters, and envelopes, which maybe they can get from their office at work. Because we are already sending out issues to people short on bread, we really do need this kind of help. We will report on all of our finances from time to time, and if you can dig it, we will probably need some kind of bail fund set up. If any YIPL busts happen, we'd like to ask you all in advance to work extra hard for the cause. People, thanks again. Love

THE CREDIT CARD CODE

The 1971 Credit Card system works as follows: The telephone number(7digits) of the number to be billed is followed by the secret number for the area code of the number. They are listed below for several cities. At the end of the number comes a letter that matches the sixth digit of the telephone number. Many people look up the number of a large Company in the area and use their number, cause using any old number might lead to that person refusing to pay, and the Phone Company's hasseling the person to whom the call was placed. They should say that others use that phone, and they don't know anything. Fraud is illegal, so we don't think you should make free calls. This Code has already been printed in many underground papers, as you know.

Detroit-083	Boston-001	Phila.-041	1=Q	4=H	7=K	0=Z
Washington-032	San Fran-158	Pitts.-030	2=A	5=J	8=U
New York-021	Chicago-097		3=E	6=N	9=W

Example- 769-1900-069-Z (I.B.M. ,Amant,N.Y.)

TECHNICAL INFORMATION

As long as you're paying a bill, the phone company will tend to let you be.
We all know that you might have extra phones you want connected as freebees.
Not Western Electric phones, of course. Remember, the phone company "frowns
upon" hooking them up yourself, so we suggest you have a friend do it.

On-hook voltage:45 V
Off-hook voltage:4.5 V
Ring pulses: 90 V

Your telephone line is usually a red and a green
wire. A yellow is sometimes used for ringing. Unscrew your storebought phone on the bottom and
you will find a box with a bunch of screws on it. Connecting as in the
diagram will activate it. Some people say disconnecting the bell on that
phone will keep it a secret from "Them".

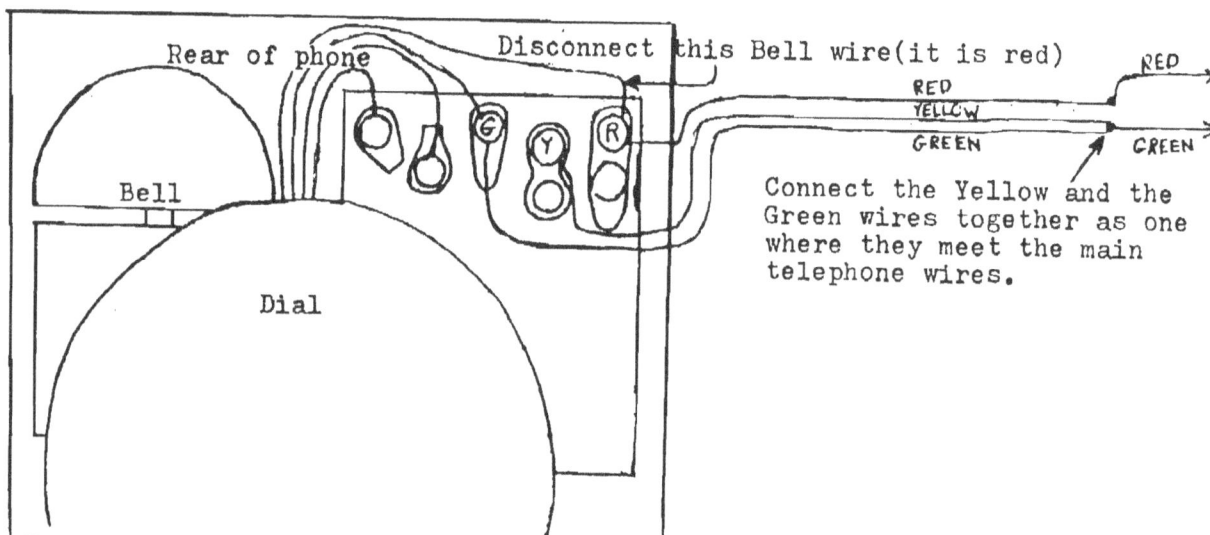

Rear of phone   Disconnect this Bell wire(it is red)   RED

RED
YELLOW
GREEN   GREEN

Bell

Connect the Yellow and the
Green wires together as one
where they meet the main
telephone wires.

Dial

Ever wonder how those conference call makers that are sold on the commercial
market work? What they do is as follows:

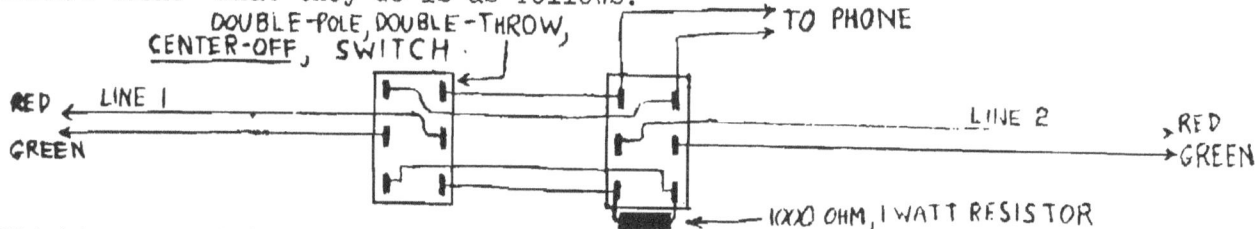

DOUBLE-POLE, DOUBLE-THROW,   TO PHONE
CENTER-OFF, SWITCH

RED   LINE 1   LINE 2   RED
GREEN   GREEN

                                        1000 OHM, 1 WATT RESISTOR

Flicking a switch up puts the phone on that number. Flicking it down puts
that number on "hold". The center position turns the number off. The
resistor keeps the line "off the hook" electrically, so if it is on hold,
you will not be able to receive phone calls on that number. Your line would
would appear "busy" to callers. Simple enough?

Yippies have been known to fool around with shit like this from time to
time without the permission of their local telephone company and even
though they usually get away with it, we at YIPL would never think of
advocating that type of irresponsible activity. You should always check
with your local phone company to pay them any extra money that you might
be responsible to them for, before ever fooling around with your phone.
The phone company is our friend, and they are here to help you.

LETTERS TO THE EDITOR

Dear phreeks,
I'm a phreeks in need of information, so I can balance the score between the Bell Kompany & the people. I enclose a dollar. Your brother in the movement-H.H., Jamestown, N.D.

My dearest sirs:
Nothing pleasures me more than ripping off Mother Bell. Please send newsletter. Enclosed is $1 U.S. Also-a question...A few friends of mine make long distance calls free from pay phone booths by holding the mouthpiece of the phone they're using up to the phone next to it so the operator hears the change jingle and makes the connection. I've tried it here in D.C. and the operator says the cash hasn't registered(which of course it hasn't). Please tell why. Thanks a lot. B.S., DuBois, Pa.

In our nation's Kapital there are the shiny new pay phones that work electronically, instead of the ding (5¢), ding-ding (10¢) or dong (25¢).New ones have only one slot for deposit, and on old ones your trick works, but hold the handset <u>close</u> to that phone!
Editor

Send me the shit and don't rip me off (please) S.M.,Winchester,Pa.

Dear Y.I.P.L.,
I thought you might be interested in a movement started here in Lancaster. The movement is to have people who wish to see our troops out of Vietnam this year call their local phone company manager and have their phone removed. The manager must be told why if it is to have any effect.Hopefully enough people will feel strongly & give up phone service to begin showing up on the profits of the phone company. This would push the phone lobbies to speak out(Bell especially) to end our continued involvement there. If you can assist in any way by encouraging this to take place in other areas it would be appreciated. Thanks! J.G., Lancaster, Pa.

Hi People,
Here's my bill, send me shit on fucking the Bell System. Man do I need info on this kinda shit thanks D.B., State College, Pa.

OUR FRIENDLY PHONE COMPANY....

One example of eavesdropping that touches a vast number of Americans was related to the Subcommittee by Joseph Beirne, President of the Communications Workers of America. He revealed that the phone company does not limit its invasions of privacy to assisting the FBI an other government tappers. He pointed out that " as part of its training program, and as part of its continuing close supervision of its employees, the telephone industry has developed equipment for monitoring its operators, its service assistants, its commercial office employees-in short, all of its employees who deal with the customer. Such monitoring means, of course, that the customer is, in effect, monitored at the same same time."
"An alert snooper is sometimes able to obtain the information he needs simply by calling the telephone office and posing as a telephone repairman. Or, if the tapper is a law-enforcement officer, her may be able to secure the outright cooperation of the telephone company in the placing of his taps. In Kansas City, the existence of just such an arrangement between the telephone company d the chief of police was revealed."
 e above two quotes were made by Senator Edward V. Long.

In the office we call it "The System", and use of the word "the" means dogmatic finality. The wall comes up pretty fast when you start tampering with the way things are done within The System, and you either slow down and do things Bell's way or knock your brains out.-AT&T junior executive,spring,1967

In April of 1966, as the government was escalating the Vietnam war, Congress passed a law raising the Federal tax on telephone service to 10%. "It is clear," said Rep. Wilbur Mills, Chairman of the House Ways and Means Committee, "that Vietnam and only the Vietnam operation makes this bill necessary". -Congressional Record, February 23, 1966.

The War Tax Resistance is showing people how to refuse to pay this war tax. In most cases, the IRS will come to collect with 6% interest, but your phone service will continue. But the more it's done, the more it costs Them in time, trouble and embarrasment for Uncle Sham. Do it, and tell your friends, relatives and neighbors to do the same. Include a letter to this effect to the phone company and your congressmen:

Date_____

BECAUSE OF THE BRUTAL AND AGGRESSIVE WAR the United States government is conducting against Vietnam, the amount of the federal excise tax, $............., has been deducted from my payment of this bill. I have opposed this war and protested against it in many ways. Now I must testify to my opposition by refusing to pay this tax.

The telephone excise tax was raised in April, 1966, only in order to help pay for the war in Vietnam. Paying the tax means helping to pay for outright atrocities, for the murder of innocent women and chidren. It means helping to pay for the indiscriminate bombing and napalming of defenseless villages. It means helping to finance the shipping of American boys half way around the world to die defending an unpopular, totalitarian and corrupt regime.

I am sorry for any inconvenience my tax refusal may cause your office and hope you will understand that this protest is not directed against the telephone company. I hope also that you will soon join me and the many others who have decided that it is now necessary to oppose the war by refusing to pay the telephone excise tax that helps finance it.

Sincerely in peace,

Distributed by
WAR TAX RESISTANCE
339 Lafayette Street
New York, N.Y. 10012

IN NEED

How do we communicate with our people serving time in Nam? WPAX has a way. They're putting rock and soul and rap and education tapes on the air through Radio Hanoi, who is donating free air time to broadcast these "subversive" sounds, now banned by our government's stations. But WPAX needs your blank and recorded tapes, and of course, bread. Send what you can. If you want to record your own show to be aired, ask them for details and they'll be happy to supply them. WPAX, Box 410, Cooper Station, N.Y., N.Y. 10003

GETTING PAST ISSUES OF YIPL

Obviously, as people join up later on, they're going to want info that was already published. So we'll have a stock of past issues, available at the ridiculous (?) price of 50¢ each. This might start to erase our deficit, but we'll lower the price if we can get enough contributions.

IN OUR NEXT ISSUE

We will have more letters, info, shit, and our man on the scene, Al Bell, will have some inside info on the "Blue Box" that people all over the country are using on Ma Bell. Plus a dialogue with Russel Baker and Abbie Hoffman on Fones.

PUBLIC ENEMY No. 1

We beg you consider donating a small percent of what YIFL helps you save.

One year of newsletters is $4.
YIPL, Room 504, 152 W. 42 St., N.Y., N.Y.

YOUTH INTERNATIONAL PARTY LINE

REVISED ISSUE NO. 2

YIPL

JULY, 1971

'Blue Box' Is Linked to Phone Call Fraud

By ROY R. SILVER
Special to The New York Times

MINEOLA, L. I., May 5—

Armed with a court order, detectives of the prosecutor's rackets bureau and telephone company personnel searched the home at 26 Henhawk Road last night. They said they found a small box measuring 5 by 6 by 3½ inches attached to a telephone in the youth's room.

The prosecutor did not say who had made the box. The telephone company said similar devices had been used elsewhere in the country before.

The telephone company became suspicious when computer cards showing the amount of time used for information calls indicated that some calls were taking much more than the usual one to three minutes.

```
1=700 + 900
2=700 + 1100
3=900 + 1100
4=700 + 1300
5=900 + 1300
6=1100 + 1300
7=700 + 1500
8=900 + 1500
9=1100 + 1500
0=1300 + 1500
KP=1100 + 1700
ST=1500 + 1700
Disconnect=2600
```

FIG. 1

FIG. 2

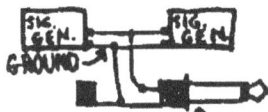

TO AUX. INPUT JACK

TO AUX. SPEAKER JACK

by Al Bell

After interviewing engineering students around the country, I found that the blue box makes tones that are similar to, but not exactly like a pushbutton phone. Since operators use the same device for putting operator-assistance calls through, the tones were published in the Bell System Technical Journal, 1960 Large libraries and engineering schools have the Journal. Like a pushbutton phone, two frequencies make up each tone. One of the "boxers" who was not caught said, "Those people who were caught probably called information, 'bleeped' out the operator, and redirected the call with the box, by pressing the buttons of the desired number. I haven't been caught because I call fro a pay phone, and I never stay on more than 15 minutes. Most imprtantly, I never use information. I use the Sheraton Hotels Watts Line number, 800-325-3535. Right before they answer, I bleep them out ".

But the blue box isn't necessary. A cassette tape machine will work fine. Two signal **generators** are needed to record the pair of tones for each digit, start, and stop. Record each digit, & you will have a master tape from which to make actual phone number sequences on other machines. One signal generator will work if you make the master on a stereo tape, and play the two channels back together as you record them on the other tape

For this to work, several rules must be followed:
-Record direct, without microphones, as in Fig. 1.
-Record as loud as possible without distortion. Watch your record meter when making tapes.
-Only use fresh batteries, and don't wear them out.
-A better speaker for playing the tones into phones is a standard telephone earpiece. Where you steal one is your problem, (its so easy) but plug it into the ext. speaker jack as in Fig.
-Each tone lasts one second, with one second between each tone. However, wait 3 seconds after "bleeping" disconnect tone. Then play KP, area code, number, and ST, in that order.
-Hold your little makeshift speaker close to mouthpiece without moving while playing tones.
-Your electronics friends and young engineers can help you get a signal generator or two to use, and they'll help you record the tones properly.
-The two frequencies of each tone must last the entire one second, and they must start and stop simultaneously.

CAUTION: YIPL does not advocate making free calls. However, YIPL doesn't believe in paying for calls, either. If caught, you may be charged with fraud and theft of services. So consider carefully whether you <u>need</u> to call long distance, and if you do,, consider whether or not you believe in <u>free speech</u>.

The Dumbest Rip-Off

By RUSSELL BAKER

Dear Abbie (Hoffman, that is):

In reading your latest work, "Steal This Book," I had just gotten to the directions for cheating the telephone company when, following your command, somebody stole the book.

I didn't finish the telephone section and—careless me!—didn't even think to make notes. I do not even remember what size washers you recommended for dropping into pay telephone coin slots to simulate the real thing. What troubles me is something more fundamental. I wonder if you have really thought out the implications of the grand philosophical idea of destroying the telephone company, which underlies your discussion of techniques.

I suggest to you that it is simply not sound, that destroying the telephone company would, in fact, be a severe blow to every member of the counter-culture.

In the first place, you must have noticed, if you have been in England, France, Italy or Bulgaria, that it is extremely frustrating trying to get along in a country with no telephone system. The English will put up with that, the French and Italians will put up with it, and the Bulgarians will have to put up with it, but you know as well as I do, Abbie, that an American, particularly if he is in the counter-culture, needs a telephone the way a monkey needs a banana.

OBSERVER

To the American counter-culturist, a telephone in the hand is as much a part of his uniform as denim, dried lentils and a coiffure from Michelangelo's Moses.

If we destroy the telephone company, who will be the first people to picket the Pentagon to demand a new telephone company? The members of the counter-culture; provided, of course, they can learn to communicate with each other without wires. A new telephone company will inevitably rise to take the place of the old evil telephone company.

There is no reason whatever to assume that the new telephone company will be like the old evil telephone company. There is every reason, on the contrary, to believe that it will profit from its predecessor's fatal errors and do things differently.

For example: Remember last summer when members of the counter-culture were telephoning each other across the continent and charging the calls to Paul Newman's credit-card number? Somebody — was it you, Abbie? — had said that Paul Newman was so angry with the telephone company that he had invited everybody in America to telephone across the continent, using his credit-card number, so that when he received the bill he could show his irritation with the telephone company by refusing to pay it.

Well, counter-culturists galore phoned long distance, and the telephone company did not become angry. Not at all. It quietly traced each call back to the telephone of origin, often rousing some parent from his parental stupor.

"Those long-distance calls made from your telephone, apparently by your child," said the patient mechanical voices, "represent fraudulent use of a credit-card number belonging to the University of Illinois and not, as the gullible believed, to Paul Newman."

"Fraudulent—?"

"The crime is punishable by imprisonment of up to five years and—"

Well, where breathes there a parent so vile that he would send his heir to Leavenworth rather than pay a piffling $300 to the telephone company?

The present telephone company is like that. It does not come knocking at the door with a truncheon and arrest warrant to haul away members of the counter-culture. It knows that money is most easily collected from people who are soft between the ears.

"Whether your child serves five years in Leavenworth is entirely up to you, as a parent. Your telephone company, sir, does not make threats."

The next telephone company is not likely to be so indulgent if it has seen the present one collapse because its bill collection y was soft-hearted. The ne elephone pany will almost surely put members of the counter-culture on trial in Chicago for fraud, possibly before Judge Julius Hoffman.

Can you really believe that the new telephone company would continue the present one's practice of saying "Sure" when somebody dials the operator in Boston and says, "I want to make $800 worth of long-distance calls to the West Coast and have it all charged to daddy's telephone in West Orange, N. J."?

My bet, Abbie, is that they're going to say, "After seeing how the old telephone company went broke because of a bunch of cheating kids, we make it a policy to call daddy first and ask if your calls are okay with him."

Is that the kind of telephone company that counter-culture really wants? A telephone company that brings daddy into the system before the calls are made, instead of presenting him with an $800 fait accompli thirty days later?

The present telephone company is the best of all possible telephone companies for the counter-culture. Destroying it would play right into the hands of Mom and Dad. Think about it next before y reach for one of those washers.

Dear folks,
I read your letter that was passed around on May Day. Please start sending me more, I'm very interested in fucking the fucking phone company. I'm mad. Well anyway, I've enclosed a cheque of 3 dollars; please find and send those little sheets as soon as possible. Thank you kindly. up the revo, K.O., Riverdale, Md.

Enclosed is $1. Could you tell me the signs of a wire tap(hollowness & clicks?).Also, do you have the plans for a device that allows you to make long distance calls free? R.F., Norfolk, Va.

My friend, there is no sure way of detecting a tap. I view the telephone as a hot line to the pork factory. As far as plans, one guy did supply them until he got busted. Using info in this issue, consult a friend on power supplies(regulated) and oscillators.

While I was in D.C. for Mayday, I picked up some info on how to fuck the Bell system. I'm really interested in this because I know how true this all is because I work in the computer room of the phone company. I'm sending $1 so that I can receive your newsletters. And if there is anything I can do for Y.I.P. just let me know. And if there's any way of fucking up the govt. in any other way, let me know. J.W., Pa.

Richard M. Nixon-El Presidente
202 456-1444
Spiro T. Agnew-El Toro
202 265-2000 Ext. 6400
John H. Mitchell-El Butcher
202 965-2900
Melvin R. Laird- El Defendo
301 652-4449
Henry A. Kissinger-El Exigente
202 337-0042
William P. Rogers-El Crapper
301 654-7125
General Earl G. Wheeler-El Joint Bosso
703 527-6119

Call collect, from a pay phone, people.

Dear Russel (Baker that is):

I just read your letter and was surprised you even saw Steal This Book since no major newspaper, including that well known spokesman for free speech, the New York Times, will accept an ad for the book. None-the-less, the boys down at AT&T must be happy to know they have a friend at the Times. It's true even us yippies don't wish to hatch our coast-to-coast conspiracies using dixie cups with waxed string stretched between them. But if our efforts to sabotage the phone company by teaching people how to make calls free are the "dumbest rip off" then AT&T itself must be engaged in the smartest rip off. Last year their revenues amounted to about 17 billion dollars, give or take a few dimes. They made a 7.6% rate of return on their bread, which in a recession is pretty damn good. To say they function as a cut throat monopoly would be understating the case. I refer you to the excellent book called "Monopoly" by Joseph C. Goulden ($.95 Pocket Books) for a devastating account of the world's largest corporation. Witness their central role in the military-industrial complex! Laugh off their defiance of citizens and governmental attempts to hold down phone rates! Smile courteously when waiting three hours to complete your next long-distance call! Nod like a robot the next time they explain how they are controlled by their shareholders and customers! To defend their efficiency only leads me to believe you never use the phone. It's a bit unfair to compare the system here to Bulgaria or Greece or even an underdeveloped nation such as England. AT&T's current assets are estimated at 50 billion dollars, which is not exactly pocket change for most countries in the world. Even so, the systems of Sweden and Denmark seem to function better, especially with the speed in which they phase out obsolete equiptment. I should also point out that Cuba has an entirely free phone system; and that, Russell, is the point of the whole monkey business of Steal This Book in general. Yippies think you judge the goodness of nations by their goals. As the level of the technological development increases, the costs should decrease with the goal being to make everything produced in a society free to all the people, come who may. Neat, huh? Until AT&T and the other corporations really become public services rather than power and profit gobblers, we'll continue to rip them off every chance we get. If you wand to discuss this further, call me up sometime. Because of all the agencies claiming to have me under surveillance, it's one of the fastest ways to speak directly to your government.

STRIKE THE WAR MACHINE

Your voice with a smile,

Abbie Hoffman

Assignment: Monitor the telephone in the suite of Senator Eugene McCarthy at the 1968 Democratic Convention. Agents reported that McCarthy had made a phone call to a "known leftist organization" offering medical help to wounded demonstrators. -Life Magazine study of Army "Intelligence"

In addition to manufacturing Princess telephones, Western Electric makes guided missiles and is a prominent member of the military- industrial complex which so frightened President Eisenhower that he warned against its "acquisition of unwarranted influence" in his farewell address. An examination of Western Electric's defense work shows that the President had ample reason for alarm. Through adept use of a technique called profit pyramiding in the defense industry, Western Electric ran up profits of 31.3 percent on its major missile contracts, while helping the Pentagon accumulate military junk that was never used. -Monopoly, by Joseph C. Goulden

Editors Note: We intend to show, through statements such as the above two, how the Bell System has become anti-human to its customers, employees, and just about everyone else. However, it should be noted that these statements are taken out of context, and do not do justice to the case. The whole story is a lot scarier that just a "profit-gobbler". Its a question of accumulation of power and securing that power. You know, great that people are being monitored, but shit, people are being slaughtered. All in the name of money. And since we give them the money, we are at fault. Stop paying and start yelling. See ya next month, phreeks.

Published for informational purposes only by Youth Hot Line Reports, Inc.

THE GOVERNMENT IS GETTING RICHER

IF WE HELP YOU TO SAVE MONEY, WE'D LOVE IT IF YOU COULD SEND US MONEY OR 8¢ STAMPS

THE GOVERNMENT PUSHES SPEED & SMACK

Coming soon-Special PAY PHONE issue.
A year of issues is $4. Who cares?
TAP, Room 418, 152 W. 42 St., N Y 10036

yipl

TO:

2

YiPL — THE YOUTH INTERNATIONAL PARTY LINE

AUGUST, '71 NO.3

YIPL PRICE CHANGE!

We are reluctant to announce a price
change because we've taken pride in
offering the best thing you could
buy for a buck. Now we're the best
thing you can buy for two bucks. It
should be obvious to anyone who takes
the time to calculate what twelve 8¢
cost us.
The price change is retroactive. If
you can't afford to shell out another
buck, it means you're just another
 exploited serf of Amerikan industria-
lism, and we'll understand. However,
···ou should know that if we don't get
  ·ough, we may have to stop printing.
Good cheer.

BELL EMPLOYEES!!!

If you are a Bell System Employee, you
know well enough just what a skinflint
company you work for. Write us your
documented experiences about working
for the largest, most powerful piece
of shit in the whole world. If you
don't work for the phone company but
know someone who does, tell them to
write us.
Other suggestions might be to post
issues of YIPL inside the telephone
building of at key places where
pissed-off workers are likely to
see it.
We want to have specific examples of
sexism, racism, anti-semitism, pigism,
and any other ism you can think of.

BACK ISSUES

STATEMENT OF PURPOSE

For those of you who don't understand
exactly who the hell we are, let me
make one thing perfectly clear. We
are not them. Now don't misunderstand
me. Of course, they could be saying
the same thing about us, but certainly
not about themselves. To set the record straight, let me remind you not
to judge someone by what he says, but
by what others don't say about what he
says about them. Thank you.

YIPL is a non-profit orgainization,
not to be confused with the other
fucking rip off orgainizations that
call themselves non-profit. We are
attempting to bridge the communications gap generated by monopolies
like THE BELL SYSTEM, and American
mass media,too. We will spread any
information that we feel cannot be
spread adequatly by other means.

YIPL is a Public Service. And we need
stamps and money. And we need your
help. Tell your friends about YIPL,
and tell them information that you
learn here that could be useful. We
don't print this shit for a privileged
few who pay their money. We send a
subscription to anyone who wants one,
even if they can't afford it. If
you attend college, make copies of
useful tidbits and distribute them or
post at strategic locations. If a
half-decent paper exists in your town,
have them spread the word. And write
us your suggestions and information
that you have.

Back issues can be ordered by sending 50¢ for each issue desired. State
number of issue.

Number One- Conference call maker, the 1971 Credit Card Code, installing
extensions.

Number two- Dialogue with Abbie Hoffman and Russel Baker. THE BLUE BOX.

LETTERS TO THE EDITOR

Please mail the Youth International Party Line for one year. Of course, I wouldn't really mess around with the ol' phone, but I'd like to see how those lousy freeks do it! M.L., Yonkers, N.Y.

Dear Abbie,
Enclosed is one dollar for the YIPL which we heard about on the July 6 Alex Bennet show.
We hope your nose feels better and that America comes out okay. Love. P.S.-We have all of your books, they're great. H.,Brooklyn, N.Y.

Friends;
Kindly use the enclosed, for a year of the Party Line so highly recommended on BAI last night by Chairman Hoffman. Thanks. A.G., New Rochelle, N.Y.

Hey, I dig what you're doing. Send me those newsletters. Incidentally, I have here two credit card no.s I'd like to share. One is that of a company whose name I don't know, but it is in N.Y.C. It's 535-6025-074A. The other is our friends at IBM, Amant, N.Y. 769-1900-069Z. You may already have one or both, but they are sent to you with fondest wishes that they can be used by the people. Right on, and write on! P.S., Baltimore, Md.

Dear Abbie, Here's a dollar for a copy of the YIP paper. If at all possible, could you send me a copy of "Steal this Book". I'm a single mother of three children and use the info on ripping off the super market(food stamps help a little but they're not free). Thank You. S.C., Corona, N.Y.

FUCK THE MAIL

Guess what, freeks? The world's biggest pusher, our own Uncle Sham, is teaming up with it's rain and shine people at Wells Fargo to supposedly stop drug abuse! This is part of its good guy campaign that was started in an attempt to discredit the whole Viet Vets against the War movement, by making middle amerika think every GI has a needle in his arm.
Anyway, we're only mentioning the post office cause it seems a lot of out mail is coming to us in strange condition, like open, empty, and mutilated. We'd like to take this opportunity to gratefully thank all those responsible. The hate they incur keeps us going.
To fight back, YIPL readers are putting their stamps 1 & 1/2 inches lower on the envelope, thus escaping the postmark. Remember, freeks, recycling will save the world. And they are SPREADING THE WORD.
Drug Abuse prevention week is scheduled for October 3-9. Yippies all over will be refusing to shoot up all junk with the U.S. Govt. inspection label on it.

Prevent drug abuse

8c

Anyone subscribing to YIPL should be aware that they are probably under observation by the FBI, the Phone Company, and their local precinct. For that reason, we strongly urge that you be wary of your telephone, because if you're doing anything that's against the LAW, that's how they'll try to get you. They've got your number.

THE PRIVATE EAR

: has recently come to our attention that a new device for invading your privacy is on the market. Called the Telecommand, this device is only an extension of what was formerly available to law enforcement officers. The Telecommand attaches to your phone internally, and whenever they want to bug your pad, they just call up and send a tone into their phone before they dial the last digit of your number. This automatically picks up your phone before it rings. Now your phone, which looks like its just sitting there hung up, is really live and listening to everything going on within earshot. When he's heard enough, he simply hangs up and your phone is back to normal.

Recently, Screw magazine revealed that Nassau County D.A. Cahn had purchased several thousands of dollars worth of surveillance equiptment, including the telecommand. And this will probably be followed by police departnents all over the country.

I don't think I have to explain in detail just how fucked up it is for a D.A. to eavesdrop on the county he is supposed to be serving. What's worse, the equiptment is paid for by county taxes, just as Federal taxes pay for the F.B.I.'s versions of the same shit.

It should be realized, however, that the Telecommand is only a remote-control extension of what the Telephone Company has been using for years. Previously, the police or F.B.I. had to listen from inside the Telephone Company building. Now they can listen from the pay booth across the street. The results are frightening. They can wait for just the right moment to break down the door and catch you smoking pot, for example.

It is believed, furthermore, that computerized networks for tapping are being set up across the count . This would mean J. Edgar himself could simply .al out your number form his office and the tap would automatically be act-ivated.

And if you don't think that they have the capability to monitor thousands of people at the same time, just remember that in a whole year, your cumulative total of phone time is probably only a few hours. Tapes stored for future reference could be quickly scanned for incriminating statements.

Clicks are only a sign of an amateur tap. Do not ever assume that your phone is safe, even for a moment.

And if you don't believe it—

Arthur S. Brewster is division security supervisor for the Southwestern Bell Telephone Company, assigned to the Kansas City office. He is a lawyer and since 1950 has had the responsibility, among other things, of assuring privacy of the hundreds of thousands of subscribers to the company's service. Brewster's relationship with the FBI was a close one; when the Long commit-tee subpoenaed him to testify, he notified the FBI's Kansas City office.

    Senator Long: Do your employees ever go with the FBI men when they were disguised as telephone employees?

    Mr. Brewster: I will put it this way. I think there were some bureau men who went with the telephone company people. They had on old clothes and those things....

    Senator Long: Do you do this for private detectives?

    Mr. Brewster: No, sir.

    Senator Long: Why not? It is a public service.

    Mr. Brewster: I would have to have a lot of explanation....

Steal This Book, vital to say the least,
can be had despite the dealer boycott.
Send $2.25 to TAP, Room 504, 152 W. 42 St.,
N.Y.,N.Y. 10036 10012

When sending in phone bills, or income
tax returns, forgetting to put a stamp
on the envelope won't hold up delivery.
So when you do such things, save 8¢.

Friends, we are starting to compile a
list for shoppers of products made by
pig industries and war-supported
companies. Send in your own list. We'll
publish the whole bunch soon.

A year's subscription is $4. Please send to: (no cash!)

TAP is YIPL's new name.

*TAP
ROOM 418
152 W. 42nd St.
N.Y., N.Y.*

PLACE STAMP HERE, NOT HERE

"I should like to ask the Senator from Utah whether the telephone company
has offered him the kind of proposal that it has offered me?

"Has the Senator had proposals made to him that he could own a telephone
building in his state and that the telephone company would make the loan
and endorse the loan to build a building in a big city in his state just
on the assurance that the Senator would give sympathetic consideration
to the company's problem, if he would go along with them, and that the
company would then build the building and endorse the mortgage loan
and engage the bank to make the loan with the probability that he would
wind up eventually being worth $5 million or $25 million?Has my good
friend ever heard the   saying,"Keep the price as high as the traffic will
bear?".

     "Did it ever occur to the Senator that he might be one of the only
members of Congress who has never had the opportunity to own a telephone building?".

               -Senator Russell Long, on the floor of the Senate.

Friends, are you disillusioned with the System? Beat it.

          Published for informational purposes only by the Technological American Party.

If a thousand men were not to pay

their tax bill this year,

that would not be a violent and bloody

measure as it would be to pay them

and enable the State to commit violence

and shed innocent blood.

HENRY DAVID THOREAU

TO:

3

SEPTEMBER '71
VOLUME 4
THE YOUTH
INTERNATIONAL
PARTY
LINE

SPECIAL PAY PHONE ISSUE

It is important that we understand the basic fundamentals of the Pay Phone before attempting to abuse this noble species.

Fig. 1 shows the standard, or "old" version. More plastic parts are used on this model, making the coin returns, for example, very attractive targets for cherry bombs. Note three slots for depositing money. A nickel, when dropped, roduces a "ding", a dime makes a "ding-ding", and a quarter, you guessed it, makes a "gong". The sounds are heard both by you and the operator when they occur. Money deposited during a call on this phone drops several seconds after you hang up, on a pulse by the operator, who can send it to you by coin return, or to them via the coin box.

Fig. 2 shows the phone the Bell people designed to eliminate YIPL. (So they thought!) To prevent us from tape recording the dings and dongs, this model uses "beeps", and you can't even hear them. BUT, if you call a friend and stick in money while you're talking, he will. Thus, he can record them.

Fig. 3 shows you how to directly record the tones from the phone at your friend's house. Using a microphone doesn't work well enough. Never play beeps into an old phone, or dings into a new one, because the operators know. Operators know the prefix (first three digits) of the phone you're on, and they know if you're at a pay phone. They know when to suspect something if you're not careful, and they sometimes put stakeouts on booths frequented by yippies. Keep moving around. See issue #17.

The polarity of the pulse the operator sends to drop coins determines where it will go. If the incoming wires of a phone you know are exposed, you can reverse the crucial two and get money back each time she tries to collect it. There are only 4 wires, and the ones to reverse are usually black & yellow or black & red. This only works till the collecting dude comes and finds the box empty. See issue #15.

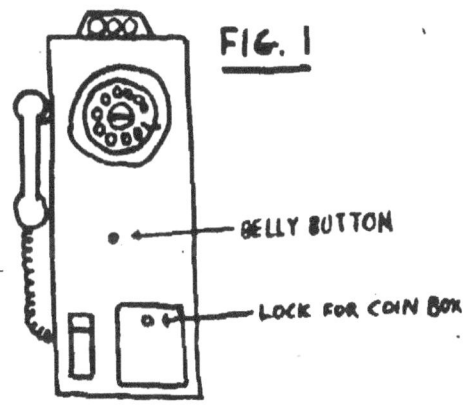

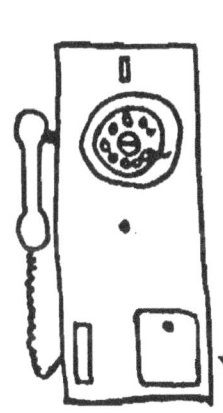

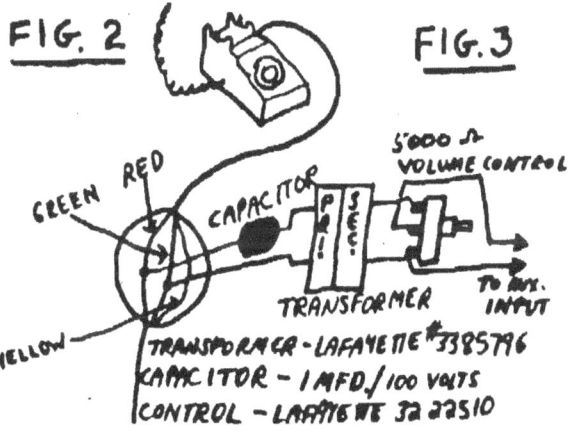

FIG. 1

— BELLY BUTTON

— LOCK FOR COIN BOX

FIG. 2

FIG. 3

GREEN RED

CAPACITOR

5,000 Ω VOLUME CONTROL

TRANSFORMER

TO AMY. INPUT

YELLOW

TRANSFORMER - LAFAYETTE #3385796
CAPACITOR - 1 MFD./100 VOLTS
CONTROL - LAFAYETTE 32 22510

abbie hoffman on pay phone justice...

"You can make a local 10 cent call for 2 cents by spitting on the pennies and dropping them in the nickel slot. As soon as they are about to hit the trigger mechanism, bang the coin-return button. Another way is to spin the pennies counter-clockwise into the nickel slot. Hold the penny in the slot with your finger and snap it spinning with a key or other flat object. Both systems take a certain knack, but once you've perfected it, you'll always have it in your survival kit.

If two cents is too much, how about a call for 1 penny? Cut a 1/4 strip off the telephone book cover. Insert the cardboard strip into the dime slot as far as it will go. Drop a penny in the nickel slot until it catches in the mechanism(spinning will help). Then slowly pull the strip out until you hear the dial tone.

A number 14 brass washer with a small piece of scotch tape over one side of the hole will not only get a free call, but works in about any vending machine that takes dimes. You can get a box of thousands for about a dollar at any hardware store. You should always have a box around for phones, laundromats, parking meters and drink machines.

Bend a bobby pin after removing the plastic from the tips and jab it down into the transmitter(mouthpiece). When it presses against the metal diaphragm, rub it on a metal wall or pipe to ground it. When you've made contact you hear the dial tone.

Put a dime in the phone, dial the operator and tell her you have ten cents credit. She'll return your dime and get your call for free. If she asks why, say you made a call on another phone, lost the money, and the operator told you to switch phones and call the credit operator.

This same method works for long distance calls. Call the operator and find out the rate for your call. Hang up and call another operator telling her you just dialed San Francisco direct, got a wrong number and lost $.95 or whatever it is. She will get your call free of charge.

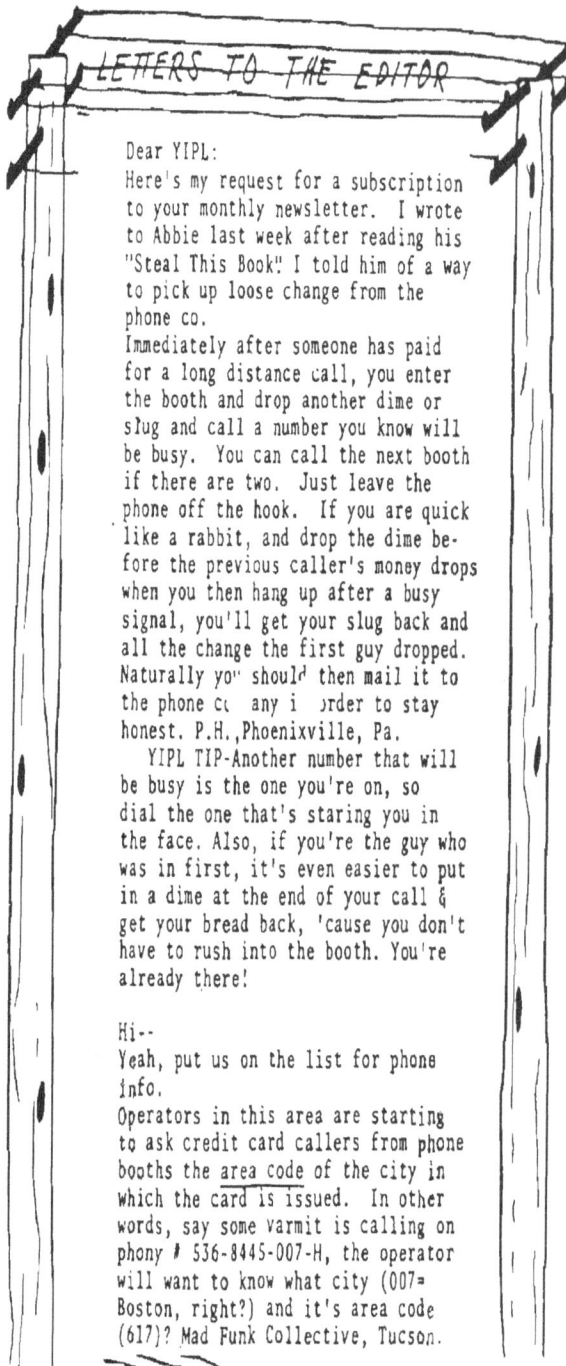

Dear YIPL:
Here's my request for a subscription to your monthly newsletter. I wrote to Abbie last week after reading his "Steal This Book." I told him of a way to pick up loose change from the phone co.
Immediately after someone has paid for a long distance call, you enter the booth and drop another dime or slug and call a number you know will be busy. You can call the next booth if there are two. Just leave the phone off the hook. If you are quick like a rabbit, and drop the dime before the previous caller's money drops when you then hang up after a busy signal, you'll get your slug back and all the change the first guy dropped. Naturally you should then mail it to the phone co any i order to stay honest. P.H.,Phoenixville, Pa.

YIPL TIP-Another number that will be busy is the one you're on, so dial the one that's staring you in the face. Also, if you're the guy who was in first, it's even easier to put in a dime at the end of your call & get your bread back, 'cause you don't have to rush into the booth. You're already there!

Hi--
Yeah, put us on the list for phone info.
Operators in this area are starting to ask credit card callers from phone booths the area code of the city in which the card is issued. In other words, say some varmit is calling on phony # 536-8445-007-H, the operator will want to know what city (007= Boston, right?) and it's area code (617)? Mad Funk Collective, Tucson.

NEWS BULLETIN: BELL-CWA TALKS AGAIN STALEMATED AS BELL COMPLAINS OF EQUIPTMENT SABOTAGE. FAR OUT!

You can make a long distance call and charge it to a phone number. Simply tell the operator you want to bill the call to your home phone because you don't have the correct change. Tell her there is no one there now to verify the call, but you will be home in an hour and she can call you then if there is any question. Make sure the exchange (prefix)goes with the area you say it does.
You can make all the free long distance calls you want by calling your party collect at a pay phone. Just have your friend go to a prearranged phone booth at a prearranged time. This can be done on the spot by having the friend call you person to person. Say you're not in, but ask for the number calling you since you'll be "back" in 5 minutes. Once you get the number, simply hang up, wait a moment and call back your friend collect. The call has to be out of the state to work, since operators are familiar with the special extension numbers assigned to pay phones for her area and possibly for nearby areas as well. If she asks you if it is a pay phone say no. If she finds out during the call(which rarely happens) and informs you of this, simply say you didn't expect the party to have a pay phone in his house and accept the charges. We have never heard of this happening though.

If there are two pay phones next to each other, you can call long distance on one and put the coins in the other. When the operator cuts in and asks you to deposit money, drop the coins into the one you are not using, but hold the receiver up to the slots so the operator can hear the bells ring. When you've finished you can simply press the return button on the phone with the coins in it and out they come. If you have a good tape recorder(cassete) you can record the sounds of a quarter, dime and nickel going into a pay phone and play them when the operator asks you for the money. Turn the volume up as loud as you can get.

MONKEY WARFARE

"If you like Halloween, you'll love monkey warfare. It's ideal for people uptight about guns, bombs and other children's toys, and allows for imaginative forms of protesting, many of which will become myth, hence duplicated and enlarged upon. A syringe (minus the needle) can be filled with a dilute solution of epoxy glue. Get

the two tubes in a hardware store and squeeze into a small bottle of rubbing alcohol. Shake real good and pour into the baster or syringe. YOU HAVE ABOUT 30 MINUTES BEFORE THE MIXTURE GETS TOO HARD TO USE. Go after locks, parking meters, and telephones."

A word about this. If someone has to make an emergency call, think of what pouring the shit down the coin slot would have done. A good way to use monkey warfare is to keep thinking, "How can I fuck the pigs, and help my sisters and brothers?" It then becomes obvious to glue the lock on the coin box, so they can't collect. And if you jam up the entrance to a parking meter slot, people can park there for free and have a ticket-saving excuse.

A year subscription of YIPL costs four dollars. TAP Room 504, 152 W. 42 St, N.Y.,N.Y. Steal This Book, if you can't get at your locality, costs $2.25 from TAP.

Back issues still cost 50¢ each. State issue number.
1- Conference call maker, '71 Credit Card code, installing extensions free.
2-Dialogue with Abbie Hoffman and Russel Baker, and The Blue Box Story.
3-The Telecommand, and a lot of assorted shit.

NEXT ISSUE: LETTERS, QUESTIONS, ANSWERS, INTERVIEWS, AND MORE.

IT SEEMS THAT PLACING STAMPS
I INCH LOWER ON AN ENVELOPE
AVOIDS A POSTMARK.

Published for informational purposes only by the Technological American Party (TAP).

4 TO:

Hang up on war

DON'T PAY PHONE TAX

Many thousands are refusing to pay the federal phone tax that goes for war. For information:

War Tax Resistance
339 Lafayette Street, New York City 10012
(212) 477-2970

CIRCULATION: 400

YIPL

DO NOT READ THIS!!

OCTOBER, 1971 VOLUME 5

YOUTH INTERNATIONAL PARTY LINE

BELL SYSTEM

ops! We must correct an error in issue
o. 2. The Start and Stop tones were
ncorrectly identified. The following
re the correct tones, guaranteed to
ork perfectly. Please, if you save
ack issues, or pass them out, change
he info on them right now.

	700	900
	700	1100
	900	1100
	700	1300
	900	1300
	1100	1300
	700	1500
	900	1500
	1100	1500
	1300	1500
tart	1100	1700
top	1500	1700
onnect		2600

7 oscillators required.

REMEMBER THE BLUE BOX?

We have received, in response to the blue box story,
requests from many people for schematics. We have
no such schematics, and would not publish them if we
did, for that would be unlawful activity.

The following is a reader-supplied schematic for
well-known phase shift oscillator. This transistor
oscillator can be operated from a 9-volt battery, but
its output is not sufficient to feed a speaker. Next
month we will show a mixing and boosting circuit for
amplification through a speaker. This circuit is useful
in the 500-5000 cycle range and as such makes an easy-
to-build, low-cost, toy organ.

C (mfd.)	frequency
.001	3000
.0016	2500
.0022	1600
.0033	1400
.0033	1200
.0044	800
.0056	600

+9Volts (Battery)

150 KΩ

5.6 KΩ → OUTPUT TO AMP

C

C   C

B   C   HEP-54 TRANSISTOR

E

22KΩ   25 or 50 KΩ TRIMPOT   22KΩ   560Ω   15 mfd. /10 V electrolytic

Notes

* All resistors are any wattage.
* Capacitors (C) should be high-quality silvered-mica, or epoxy. Disc type are poor!

o —9 Volts (Battery)

LETTERS + ANSWERS

Yea!
They've been fucking us over good. We owed them a hunk-a-money and after endless arguments with their machine ladies (strangely loyal for low down clerks) we agreed to mail them the money. They screamed back- No, we want you to bring it down in person tomorrow! What fuckers! This country's gotten too dependent on them. Send all the anti-phone shit you got. E.I.,Wash.,D.C.

Questions:
1-How can I get around paying a $50 installation deposit?
2-How can an extra line be installed?
3-Is it easy to get electrocuted if you have a phone in the bathtub and it falls in?
4-Credit card #'s of environment-destroying companies(oil, chemical).

You can only get a free extra line if you know someone in your local exchange who can pull it off. If you're daring, extend your neighbor's wires from where they connect into his house. If you are living in a college dorm or apt., ask a friend if you can use his/her line, & run a 2-conductor wire to your conference switch(issue no. 1). If you don't have any friends where you live, and you need an extra outgoing line, the junction box is a good access point to other lines. Usually, the lines all connect from outside to the individual rooms in this box or mini-closet. The lines connect via 4-conductor cable, 2 conductors of which are used. The remaining two are cut off or wrapped around the cable in the box, and are present in the wall box in your room. Connect your spare pair to some straight's line, and in your room connect to a conference switch. When he goes to sleep at 11 on the dot, you're free to call out on his number. Don't leave the box connected up that way all the time or someone might spot it on a check.

We doubt a phone can electrocute you in a bathtub, but since they're not allowed to install a movable phone in a bathroom, take a tip and mount your phone somehow.

When some readers send us a few tested numbers, we'll print them. And if anyone knows how to get away without paying the deposit, write us.

...If you're well off, Surplus Center, Lincoln, Nebraska 68501 has phones, test sets(good for tapping),switchboards. Write for catalogs.

I got my phone free. Phones for sale at Radio shack, Lafayette, Allied Radio, etc., aren't Western Electric or new looking, but they're OK. Next time you see a phone man talk awhile, then ask if you can set up an intercom with a phone that he'll "lose" from his truck. I got free a new decorator color phone. Most don't mind.
-A reader

YIPL TIP- Go into a big pig hotel sometime if you need a phone. They have them in lobbies for calling within the building. If they're in a bad location, go up a few flights. They probably'll have them in the hall near the elevator. Bring a knife or scissors, and a shopping bag.

Although there are some cool phone repairmen around, many are to be feared. If you have a repair or installation visit, don't leave dope, non-Bell phones, or subversive literature just lying around, or he may report you to his supervisor for suspicion. That may result in a bust, through cooperation with the local precinct, or a tap on your line. This isn't paranoia, it's fucking good sense.

Brothers and Sisters,
Need your help on a special project for our news collective here in Houston...I am planning a documentary special on phone phreaking and related subjects and need as much info as is possible...Could you please send me what info you have and possibly the adresses of other phone phreaks, and can you relay my intentions into the phone phreak network and if they can help me they can call me here at Pacifica 713-224-4000, no collect calls please I'm poor as hell. But if they can call me via phone phreaking network so I can tape interviews, demonstrations, and other such shit I would be eternally grateful....POWER! Scoop Sweeney,Arch fiend,pervert, degenerate, and sometimes newsman. KPFT,618 Prairie, Houston, Texas 77002

Church Withholds Phone Tax

The congregation of Hollis Unitarian Church escalated its protest against American war policies yesterday by not paying the federal excise tax portion of the church's monthly telephone bill.
- "The war, and only the war, makes this tax necessary," said the church's minister, the Rev. F. Allen Wells Jr. "It has become, more than any other tax, symbolic of the war."

WAR TAX RESISTANCE
339 Lafayette Street
New York 10012

CAROLINA PLAIN DEALER RIPOFF

TICK CREEK, NC (CMC)- American Telephone and Telegraph, one of the largest war contractors
i oppressor of millions of employees is trying its hand at censorship of the underground
press. Three staffers and one hawker of the CAROLINA PLAIN DEALER have been charged with
"providing information for the theft of telecommunication service," a 6 month and/or $500
misdemeanor. The February PLAIN DEALER contained the commonly known information of how
the telephone credit card system works. The bust is an attempt to intimidate the free
press and possibly to regain some of AT&T's billions lost on fake credit card calls. But
they have lost even more by this attempted ripoff of the DEALER staff. They hired two
full-time special security investigators who spent two months traveling around the Carolinas tracking us down. They followed and harrased hundreds of highschool and university
students during their investigations. They have subpoened two witnesses: a young HS woman,
and a college student caught making credit card calls. Schools cooperated fully with the
private pigs. People were dragged out of classes and questioned by the principal and the
telephone pigs.

The first attempt at a "trial" was postponed by the state because they have not been able
to locate our printer. Thirty beautiful people from all over the Carolinas ignored the boring
trial proceedings and picniced in the courthouse hall, sang and danced before the astonished
pigs.

The next trial date has not been set. We are gathering information to prove that some of
their evidence is based on an illegal phonetap.

It took the state and local pigs three months to find us all. One of us spent three weeks
in a woodland hideout while the $1000 bond was being secured.

We live in rural North Carolina. One of the pigs that was visiting us while looking for
the fugitives said "If you people don't break it up out here we're going to have to arrest
you for cohabitation, fornication, and adultry." We wanted to tell him none of us were
married.

If convicted, the implications are not clear. AT&T may attempt busts of other newspapers
other areas. But they lose no matter what they do if we exploit the contradictions. (Now
they have to prove in court that they have the right to charge for public service). The district telephone manager who signed the warrant is quoted as saying 'We definitly see ourselves
as the establishment." *call anywhere ... but dial with care*

HOW NOT TO GET CAUGHT MAKING FAKE CREDIT CARD CALLS

Bell Telephone, subsidiery of AT&T with 1970 assets of $49.6 Billion, the world's big-
gest pig corporation, is losing millions monthly on fake credit card calls. They are not
taking it lightly. Their methods of attempted repression would make the FBI proud. Here's
how they work it.

First, the phone company sometimes makes the operator that took a fake credit call attempt to trace the caller. They tell her/him that they will take the cost of the call out
of their salary if she doesn't try to find out who made the call. The operator will call
the number that you placed the call to, attempting to track you down. Obviously only make
credit card calls to people you trust not to reveal your identity. When an operator calls
you inquiring about a credit card call, have a story ready. If she (or he) sounds friendly,
use a story like, "I only know their first name was George and he was calling from Boston,
operator." If a nasty supervisor bitch calls, be nasty offensive. You don't have to give
out any information. Usually they want to know whose name the number is listed under. Let
them find out the hard way. Sometimes they ask if your mother is home. Sometimes they
guess who called and bill them by examining the past accounts of the person called to see
who has called previously from the same city as the credit card call was made from. Sometimes they bill the number called. Sometimes they put it on the bill as a third party charge
or a collect call. REFUSE TO PAY. Keep track of the calls you actually do make and the
credit card calls you receive (so you can refuse to pay them).

If the operator gets a lead to who made the credit card call, she turns the name over to
the telephone security division. They have special security pigs that can spend their full
time tracking us down. They will stop at nothing. They stakeout phone booths; don't always
use the same location to call from. In some states they are allowed to tap your phone if
there is a case of "defrauding the phone co." And of course they tap phones in all states
whether they are allowed to or not. Their easist victims are highschool and university

people. They investigate with the cooperation of the school pigs. In high schools they work with the principal. They call the suspected person into the office and give her/him the third degree, promising not to prosecute if they will tell the pigs everyone else making credit card calls. Divide and conquor it's called. At universities, the special telephone security pigs work in conjunction with the campus cops. They may follow you around and attempt to question you. YOU DO NOT HAVE TO TELL THEM ANYTHING! Refuse to talk without your lawyer present. Above all, do not sign anything. They try to get you to sign a confession just like in the movies. Don't be intimidated by these junior facists! Throw tomatoes at them; put sugar in their gas tanks. All power to the imagination!

The way we make credit card calls is as important as knowing the system. Operators take many real credit card calls daily and know what the average call sounds like. The average caller is Mr. or Mrs. Pig Businessperson. They come on fast and usually have the number memorized. It sounds suspicious if you sounds suspicious if you sound like you are reading it off, or if you say, "841 dash 7767 dash 167N." The beginning numbers are a phone number and should be read as "841 7767" with the last part read as a single unit, 167N. A good opener is, "Operator, credit card call. My number is 893 4452 359J. The number I wish to call is 777-8787." Don't hesitate, memorize your credit card number, and have all the info handy.

Do not call from your home phone. When making a credit card call, you do not have to give the operator the number you are calling from. If she asks, change the last digit or two. Operators usually only know the prefix you are calling from. She may say hold on, and call the number you give to see if it's busy. So if you call from a pay phone, which you should, give her the number of your pay phone, it's cool.

The July 16 (issue 104) BERKELEY TRIBE has much more good info on telephone procedures in ripoffs!

BACK ISSUES cost 50 cents each. Think about it.

No. 1- Credit card code, installing conference lines and free extensions.
No. 2-The Blue Box Story, dialogue with Abbie Hoffman and Russel Baker on Phones.
No. 3-The Telecommand, and other shit.
No. 4-Special Pay phone issue.

Confucious say; "Those who receive YIPL should have small mouth when on telephone."

Now that you're done with this issue, please pass it on to a friend, or post visibly.

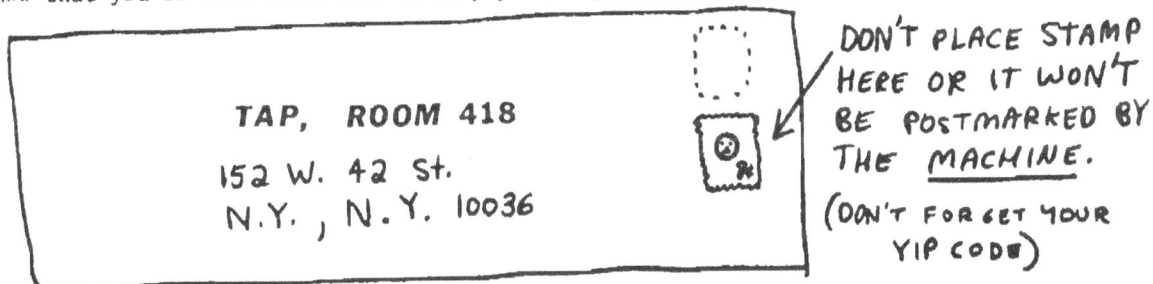

TAP,   ROOM 418
152 W. 42 St.
N.Y. , N.Y. 10036

DON'T PLACE STAMP HERE OR IT WON'T BE POSTMARKED BY THE MACHINE.
(DON'T FORGET YOUR YIP CODE)

TAP, 152 W. 42 ST, ROOM 418, NY 10036

Don't Pay War Taxes

5

CIRCULATION 500+

YIPL

VOLUME 6
NOVEMBER '71

YOUTH INTERNATIONAL PARTY LINE

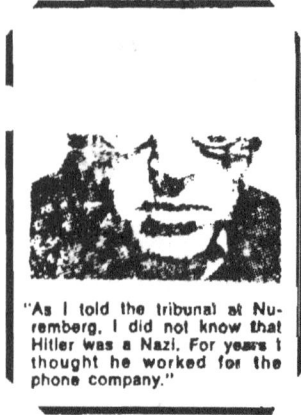

"As I told the tribunal at Nuremberg, I did not know that Hitler was a Nazi. For years I thought he worked for the phone company."

STATEMENT OF PURPOSE

A few of you have written us asking if the Esquire article is factual. It is. However, some numbers have been changed to protect the innocent. For example, the loop numbers have been changed by the telephone company. And they may change others because of the article. But the box works, and the explanation the Esquire article gives is correct. Including when they say that calling information from a home phone and using a box is not wise. If you want to make a box like Gilbertson's, see letter's column.

Some readers have been having trouble using the blue box tones on pay phones. One reason is that an intercepting operator might hear the tones and suspecting a malfuc
the tones and suspect a malfunction in the equiptment(a common occurence). She then cuts you off. You don't however, always run into an intercepting operator. If you dial long distance information(area code, 555-1212) or if you call late at nite you usually have a better chance of getting through. Also realize that the fucked-up phone system cannot handle all the calls in the U.S. on certaing nights. Friday, Saturday, Sunday, and Monday all suck. Expect to get a busy signal or operator recording on these nights.
A box works better on a home phone, but it is of course more dangerous that way. Next time your relatives invite you over, call from there and they'll never get hassled for one call, if the phone company even manages to trace it. An old couple won't be charged with using a box if you connect onto their wires in an apartment building basement. Always use an 800 number, like 800-243-1111 when calling on a non-pay phone. But please, don't call on your own line. That's asking for trouble.

Here we go again. The YIPL idea is limited if the research is left up to the staff. If our readers send in information that would be useful to other readers, and that means any information, related to phones, food, entertainment, transportation, or anything, then we would pretty soon have a centralized information pool that would be incredibly well-stocked with useful hints. We want this paper to be totally reader-supplied soon. So if you want to help with this project, all you have to do is send your idea to YIPL,Room 504, 152 W. 42 St., NY, NY. 10036. All useful ideas will be published. Announcements of new publications and events are also welcome. So get those cards and letters coming in.

THE FOLLOWING IS A RECENT COMPILATION OF CREDIT CARD CODES BY AREA.   (1972)
Atlanta 035
Detroit 096,083
Minneapolis 126
Connecticut 020
NYC 072,074,021
North. N.J. 091,094
Houston 151
Los Angeles 182
San Fran. 158
Wash.,D.C. 032
Boston 001
Chicago 097
Philadelphia 041
Pittsburgh 030

Nixon's law firm- 337 0042 023H

LETTERS TO THE READERS

Dear Youth:
Hope you enjoyed the article in Esquire. Technical details for the small machine will follow in either the Realist or Sun Dance.
-Al Gilbertson
--And in YIPL, of course.-Ed.

Dear YIPL:
Here's another tip for ripping off Bell. Suppose you open up a joint called Dope Specialties, and you want the business phone listed under that name. Upon checking with local business office you learn that they want to rip you off for a 25 dollar deposit plus 12 dollars a month.
Do this: first have the phone listed as a personal phone-8 bucks a month. Then write the pigsness office and say you have a foriegn student from Afghanistan living with you for a year and you want an additional list-ing for him. (They cost 50¢ monthly). His name is specialties dope, and lo and behold the telephone listing comes out last name first as Dope Specialties 102 dollars a year instead of 169. Another idea; rip off a repairman's handset or get a friend to do it.

You can hook into anyone's phone terminals on the outside of their house, or apartment building and dial away. You can also use them on bare terminals which are in most outside phone booths. You can only dial locally or get an operator this way, but place a long distance call and when the operator asks for the money drop it into the phone and let her hear the dings (only works on old style ones) cause you can get the money back by pushing the coin return. If you are really cool, carry the handset when you travel and just climb any telephone pole and connect in and dial away.
By the way, stay cool on the blue boxes, they are starting to crack down and many phreaks have been busted.
Another idea-it's time for new telephone books now. Check into working to help deliver them. At the distribution site(a boxcar on a railroad station) someone is supposed to check every-one who takes books, but no one does. A VW full of books gets $10 here at the Junk Com-pany for paper salvage. Last year I knew

two dudes who got 34 van loads in 2 1/2 d. work. That's an easy 340 dollars. Best to make sure you got a dishonest junk man-most of them are though. -T.M.,Arlington, Va.

Dear YIPL,
Just got your newsletter today, far fucking out. I hope you keep up the good work. A good way to fuck up a pay phone is as follows; Take the pin off the back of a YIPPIE! button and turn the dial all the way around, stick the pin into the little hole (see arrow), press down hard on the pin and turn the dial clockwise, and the dial comes right off. YIPPIE!C.T.,N. Kingstown, R.I.

Dear YIPL,
Here's a supplement to that pay phone dial ripoff. Heat the pin point for about 3-5 seconds with a lighter or match; It will make it simpler to push thru the hole. And instead of removing the pin from the back of the but-ton simply bend it up and use the button as a handle. And when you get the dial off put all kinds of revolutionary slogans on the paper number disc or make up your own.
Here's an idea for all the beginning YIPL . Check the obituaries in the local papers for dead single people, then find their phone number, and call like crazy giving the deceas-ed's phone number to the operator. Make sure the stiff doesn't have a family. They have enough to worry about without being bugged by the phone company. If a person dies after the phone bills come out you have a full month before the company catches on. Fuck the System. C.T., N. Kingstown, R.I.

-Good ideas. Also put working credit card numbers on the dial paper to help out people who visit that booth. You might also want to write YIPL's address down.

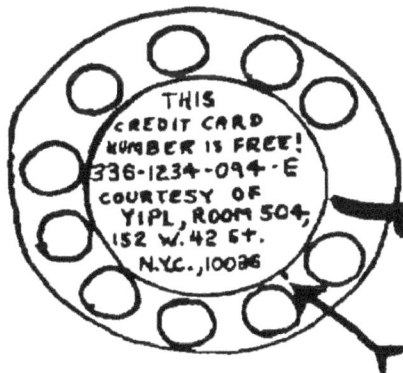

THIS CREDIT CARD NUMBER IS FREE! 336-1234-094-E COURTESY OF YIPL, ROOM 504, 152 W. 42 St. N.Y.C.,10036

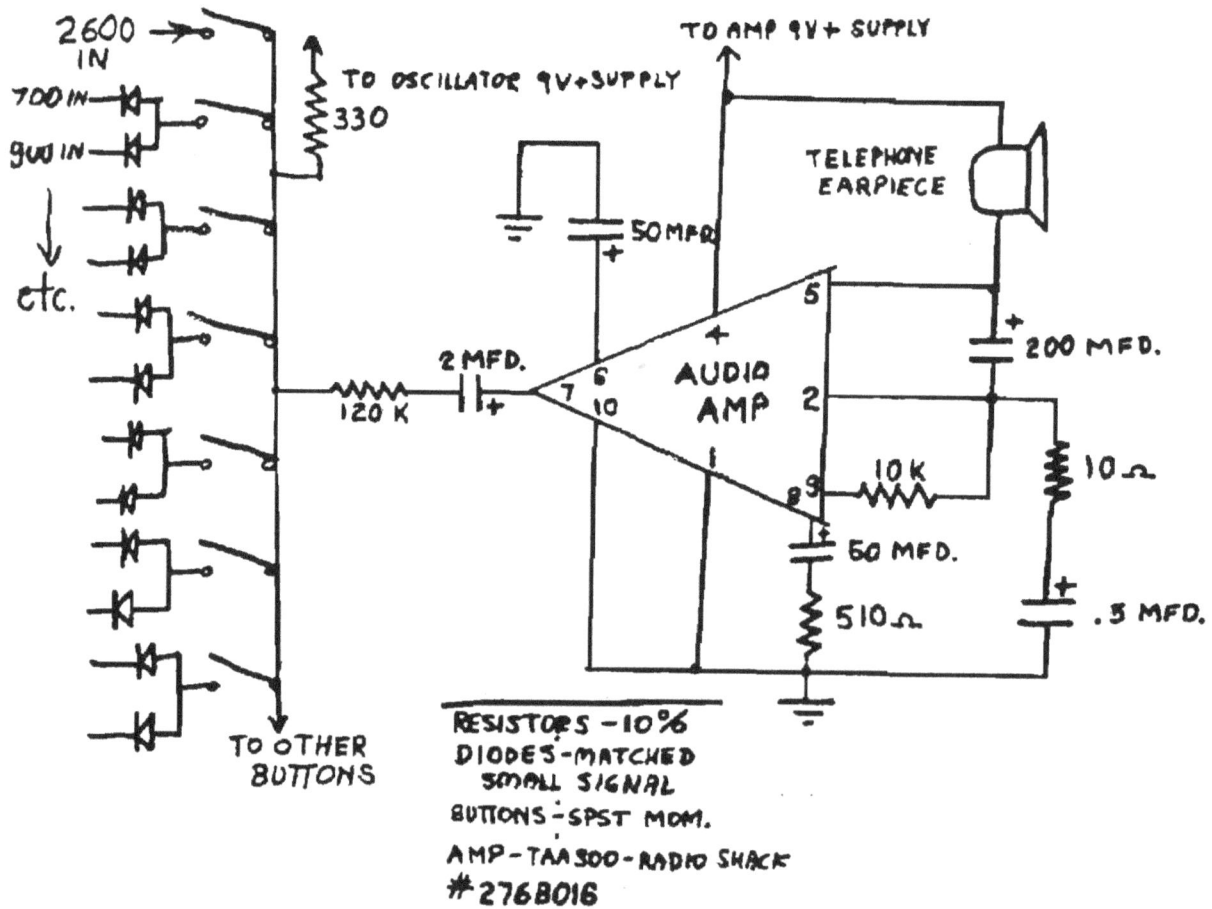

Schematic labels

2600 IN

700 IN

900 IN

↓

etc.

TO OSCILLATOR 9V+ SUPPLY

330

TO AMP 9V+ SUPPLY

TELEPHONE EARPIECE

50 MFD

2 MFD.

120 K

AUDIO AMP

7 6
   10

5

2

8 3

200 MFD.

10 Ω

10K

50 MFD.

510 Ω

.5 MFD.

TO OTHER BUTTONS

RESISTORS -10%
DIODES-MATCHED
SMALL SIGNAL
BUTTONS-SPST MOM.
AMP-TAA300-RADIO SHACK
#276B016

NOTES

This mixer-amplifier uses 24 diodes to produce 12 separate tone pairs without mixing them at their source. Each diode is silicon, low current, and the pair should be matched if possible. A single pure tone needs no diodes, of course.

A telephone earpiece is a perfect, low cost speaker for this unit, and has the added advantage of coupling tightly with a telephone mouthpiece if you want to play this instrument to your friends, over the phone.

A 50K ohm trimmer tunes each oscillator. All parts in this project are 10% or better tolerance, but the capacitors should be drift-free types(mylar, epoxy, or mica), or else the oscillators will detune easily.

Two batteries are recommended for ease of construction and stability of tone.

This simple mixer and amplifier can be used in the electronic organ de-scribed last issue. 1) Power to the speaker will be lost at low frequencies if a suitable enclosure is not used. A small metal or plastic box is fine. The box can, of course, contain the rest of the parts. Tones can be found for suitable notes in any sound engineering manual.

2) If played into the phone for any reason, the speaker should be lined with a circle of foam to form a good seal that is held tightly to the mouthpiece.

BECAUSE OF THE BRUTAL AND AGGRESSIVE WAR the United States government is conducting against Vietnam, the amount of the federal excise tax, $.............., has been deducted from my payment of this bill. I have opposed this war and protested against it in many ways. Now I must testify to my opposition by refusing to pay this tax.

The telephone excise tax was raised in April, 1966, only in order to help pay for the war in Vietnam. Paying the tax means helping to pay for outright atrocities, for the murder of innocent women and chidren. It means helping to pay for the indiscriminate bombing and napalming of defenseless villages. It means helping to finance the shipping of American boys half way around the world to die defending an unpopular, totalitarian and corrupt regime.

I am sorry for any inconvenience my tax refusal may cause your office and hope you will understand that this protest is not directed against the telephone company. I hope also that you will soon join me and the many others who have decided that it is now necessary to oppose the war by refusing to pay the telephone excise tax that helps finance it.

Sincerely in peace,

WAR TAX RESISTANCE
339 Lafayette Street, New York, NY 10012
Phone (212) 477-2970 or 777-5560

☐ I would like to join War Tax Resistance.

☐ I am not ready to join WTR, but please place me on your mailing list.

☐ Please send me more information about the following methods of war tax resistance:

☐ Please send me _____ additional copies of A Call To War Tax Resistance (6 for 25¢; 30 for $1).

☐ I am already resisting war taxes (on a separate sheet please list the taxes you have not paid, since which year, the consequences to date, and any other pertinent information).

☐ You may use my name in publicizing WTR.

☐ I am interested in forming a WTR Center; please send me more information.

Enclosed is $ _____ to support the work of WTR. Please send copies of this Call to the attached list of people.

Name _____

Address _____

_____ Zip _____

Telephone _____

Throughout the United States, young people by the hundreds of thousands are rebelling in disgust and anger against the squandering of resources on war, and neglect **6** of the day-to-day practical needs of the people. They are not alone in seeing only massive social disruption and probably nuclear war as eventual consequences. They are risking their freedom, careers and often their lives to protest and resist what they see to be wrong.

We, as participants in War Tax Resistance, are resolved to confront our own complicity in war, waste and callousness. We resolve to end, to the extent we can, our cooperation with a federal tax program geared to death more than life.

BACK ISSUES
1-Credit card code, installing extensions and conference lines free.
2- The Blue Box story, dialogue with Abbie and Russel Baker.
3- The Telecommand.
4-Special Pay phone issue
5-Building an electic organ,Pt. 1,making credit card calls safely.

Back issues are 50¢ each. Let us know what number issue you want.

Save this paper or give it to a friend. Better yet, xerox the blue box article, or the organ plans(1 & 2) and pass them out at demonstrations. Bring YIPL info into your nearest head shop and visibly. Make sure your local underground newspaper knows about YIPL. Copies of YIPL make excellent party favors and double as napkins and rolling paper.

Write for a subscription to YIPL,Room 504, 152 W. 42 St.,NY,NY, 10036. Send us $4.00, more if you can, less if you can't.

DON'T FORGET YOUR RIP CORD.

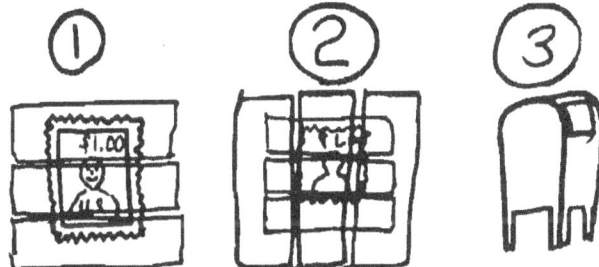

① COVER STAMP WITH TAPE, STICKY PART UP.

② COVER TAPE WITH TAPE, STICKY PART DOWN.

③ MAIL TO YIPL.

THIS IS ONLY MEANT AS AN EXPOSÉ. DO NOT DO THIS, IT IS ILLEGAL, BECAUSE IT IS FREE.

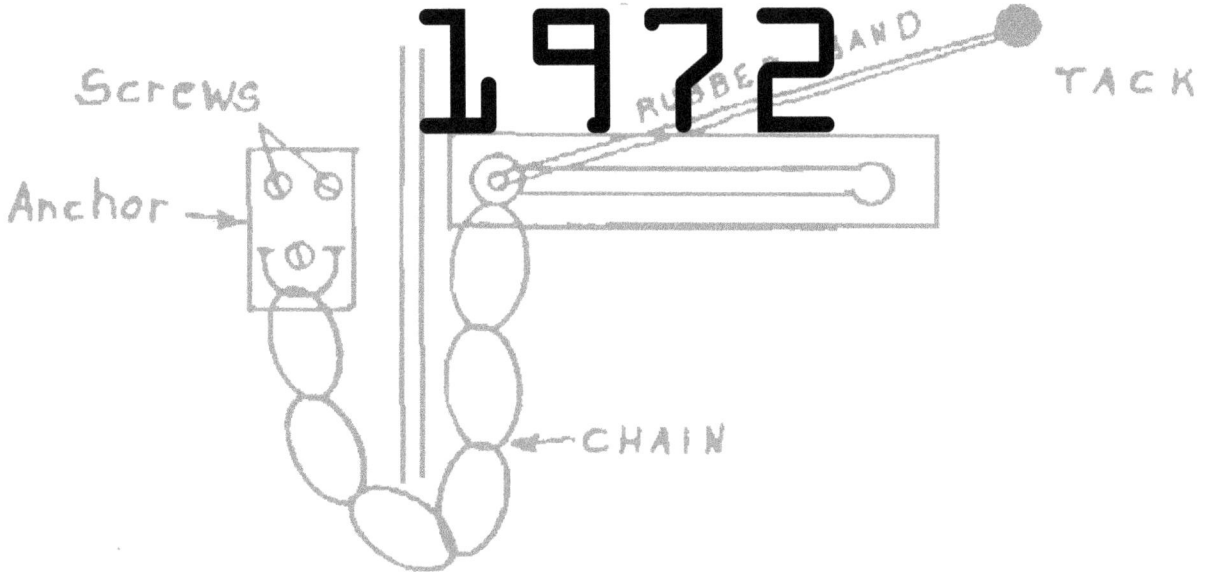

Issue #7

Dec.-Jan. '72

CIRCULATION 500

"A Wealth of Slime" YOUTH INTERNATIONAL PARTY LINE

1972 CREDIT CARD CODE

We don't have it yet. But as soon as one reader breaks the code and lets us know, you'll all know. So get friendly with an operator, apply for a credit card, or check your local underground paper. When you've got it, send it in. You are the source of our information.

The Source catalog, coming out in issues starting now, is for people who need a radical yellow pages. Source is primarily your aid to obtaining information, and it lists periodicals, documents, and even organizations like YIPL. If you're an organizer, you need Source.

Our demented readers have been deluging us with requests for suppliers of #14 brass washers. We want to know where these items can be mail-ordered from, so we can publish an expose' of such a dastardly corporation that would sell slugs good in pay phones, drink and food machines, laundromats and parking meters. So if any of you people run across such a scummy outfit, be sure to alert YIPL as to the adress ,and the price of the washers.

We have recently been advised that a seemingly outasight deal is a gyp. The Book Clubs, who advertise in the New York Times every Sunday(Book Review Section) don't tell their customers that the books come with untrimmed pages that look like shit. For this unspeakable crime, we urge YIPL readers to order the four free books(or 4for a buck) and to refuse to pay if they come with untrimmed pages. Only order from companies that do not require a signature..Also, continue ordering for weeks afterwards for all our friends if they refuse to remedy this despicable situation. And if you can believe it, The Book of the Month Club says"These books are identical to the publishers editions, ...in quality." WHat a fucking lie.

Yipl readers! We are being attacked! The U.S. Government is undermining our correspondence, and stealing your money. This is happening all the way down the line to the postmen who look through your mail before they decide to deliver it to you or not. Don't mail letters to YIPL with your local mailman. Drop them in a mailbox.Only send checks to YIPL,not cash. And most of all, place your stamps 1 1/2 inches lower on the envelope. And don't forget the zip code. We can't allow them to have an excuse for confiscating our mail.
As long as this communications gap exists, we have to ask you to help. If your YIPL gets through, Xerox it and distribute it at head shops,at clothing stores, colleges, riots, conventions, to friends,hitchers, schools.This is vital for reaching the masses whom the Government fears. One reader suggested labels that stick to phones, subway doors,etc., that have useful information about freebies.

Happy New Year to all our friends, especially the New York Tel. Co. striking workers.
1972 will provide fun for many yippies in San Diego this summer. See you there.

YIPPIES: In case you're bored one night, call Miss Weston (collect) and tell her you would like to join Diners Club. 212-245-1500.

Back issues are 50¢ each.
1. Installing extensions.
2. Blue Box Story.
3. Telecommand(story)
4. Pay phone issue
5. Organ plans(1)
6. Organ plans(11)

Y.I.P.L.-
This establishment fuck is beautiful,
it has worked everytime,for everyone.
It will work especially well now
around Christmas time. Just go into
a large store, pick something off the
shelf(packaged) and quickly walk over
to the cashier and tell her you would
like to return this item. Since you
have no sales slip(you received this
as a gift and already have one) the
sales girl will give you a merchandise
credit and you're free to look around
and choose anything your crooked little heart desires. Also,if its extra
cash you want & need, save sales slips
when you do shop and after Christmas
do the same thing as above but now
you have a sales receipt-make sure its
for the same amount please-so the
cashier will give you cash if you
can't find anything you want to exchange it for. Its really a rush!
Remember,Always Look,Act and Speak
Confident!Love and peace from K&B,
Florida.

Dear YIPL,
My name is   ,presently
I am being held prisoner by Monroe
State Reformatory, hopefully not for
very damn longer,it's hard telling
because I am on appeal,who knows how
long they can take on a appeal these
days.
Several months ago I mailed you some
stamped envelopes, so that I could get
onto your mailing list. Well, low and
behold I received an issue today, and
I find it extremely interesting,I received November's issue #6. I am going
to try to send you a few more stamped
envelopes with this letter, they are
about the only assets I have right now
and I'm pretty broke to tell the truth.
The State "gives" us three stamped
envelopes a week, and so you get to
saving them up for trading and such,
but it takes a while. So I hope that
they come to use for you.
I was wondering though,if it would be
possible to send me any back issues,
I sure would appreciate it. I can dig
finding out about installing phones,
in and around and under different conditions.

(continued in fourth column)

Dear Sir:
I have a problem which you might be
able to help with. The series of events
went like this:
1. A friend gave me a phone credit card
number and said it was O.K. to use.
2. I used it for about 3 months,making
some person to person calls(the friend
who gave it to me said to keep the
costs down that way).
3.On Nov. 23, Ohio Bell called my friends
and coaxed them into saying that I was
the person who called them from this
area.
4. The next day the phone company called
me and explained that the card was
invalid. They then said that I should
pay for the calls. When I declined, they
said they would forward the matter to
their securities dept.
If you could,please advise me on what to
do,since I don't want to pay for all
those calls.D.G.,Painesville,Ohio
-Try this: Contact your friends and
tell them to change their story if the
phone company calls them again. They
should say that "many people use this
phone operator" and they wish they
could help but they can't. When the
phone company contacts you again, de.
the charges. By the way, don't use a
credit card no. for more than a month,
or call friends who will buckle under
a threat that the phone company will
more than likely not carry through.

Yipl-For 25¢ you can get a copy of
The Daily Block also known as the
P 'lder Denver Colorado Pornography
C de & Rape the Earth, with a spec-
ial telephone section by HANG UP,A
GLOBAL COMMITTEE TO STOP AT&T.Address
is 1921 21st Street,Boulder, Colorado.
90302. It has a nice spirit.

Dear Friends:
In your pay phone issue you suggest
that a proper way to fuck a pay phone
is to glue the coin slots or the coin
box lock with epoxy glue and to use
a syringe. Excellent injectors for this
type of work can be purchased from the
Brook Stone Company. 12 for $4.95 plus
.90 postage. They look like syringes
with a needle. The order number is
Z-1135.3 and the address is
Brookstone Company
Dept. C
9 Brookstone Building
Petersborough,N.H. 03458
A good pair of bolt cutters can be had
from Brookstone. It's 14" long, easy to
hide under a coat or pants leg. They
cost $8.95 plus $1.15. I have a pair and
t⁺ ⌄ cut armored cable like string.
    Can any of you send me some #14
brass washers or an address where I
can send for some? I can't seem to find
em up here.
N.Y. Times Dec. 8,1971

Baboon in South Africa 'Takes Over' Phone System

CAPETOWN (AP) — Sub-
scribers at Kloof Nek Forest
were left to wonder about the
new bug in the telephone system when bells rang for no
reason and some heard only
barks, growls and sucking
sounds.

A baboon had gotten into the
unattended exchange. It pulled
instructions from the wall,
pressed every button on the
switchboard, spilt milk on the
floor and finally ate the only
pen of Michael Anhauser, the
operator who had left for a few
minutes.

"I don't know what to put
in my report," Mr. Anhauser
said.

It seems like we're everywhere. Keep
up he good work. C.T
-k...ember, gang, epoxy the coin boxes
only.-Ed.

I have one little idea, that I remember from way back, and so it is very
possible that you may already know
it. If you tear about a half inch
wide strip from the telephone book,
in a pay booth,and tear it so you have
a half by ten inch strip of cardboard,
you then take it and slip it down
the quarter slot in the phone, and
just drop a penny down the slot and
pull the cardboard from the phone,
but do it very slowly, and you might
try even jiggling it a bit when you
do it,once you get the hang of it it
is easier than shit, and you can call
long distance the same way, when the
operator asks you to put the money in,
just drop in your pennys into the
nickel slot, wiggle the cardboard in
the quarter slot, and it rings up the
bread, it might sound like a big
hassle, but it really isn't at all.
Well, guess I will close now, thanks
again, I really like issue#6 and think
that something of this sort should .
have come out ages ago,especially when
I was on the streets, I could have
dug getting in to it then. Also, if
you can,will you send me an extra copy
of your back issues? You may have
sent them to me already, and the pigs
here could have intercepted them, but
I think if you mail just one issue at
a time, that they will come through
OK, at least I will let you know what
happens,thanks again. In love and
peace for all, John Doe
Abby Hoffman,
Here are a few sure-fire ways to rip
off Maw Bell. On the three slot pay
phones there is a plastic case on the
bottom, underneath the phone. Now when
you unscrew the center screw it will
reveal 4 screws with a wire behind
each. Now you take the bottom right
screw and unscrew it enough to take
the wire out. Now you take the wire
and touch it to the top right wire and
presto-you got a dial tone. Call away.
A way you can get money is to unhitch
the bottom right wire and put some
tape around it so it doesn't touch any
other part. Now the phone doesn't work
but the people don't know this so they
put money in and nothing. So you come
back in a week and take the tape off
and put the wire back under its screw,
hang up the phone and you hit the jack
pot-money-money-money. (P.S.if it don't
work just push the coin return but
the above will work so you don't have
nothing to worry about). M.R., Hadley,
                                    Mass.

Tuning Your Organ

Probably one of the hardest parts of constructing our toy organ is finding a tuning method. One proven method is to use an electric organ. However, many of these are unstable and may have drifted. The Hammond B3 or C3 is a good instrument to use. With the highest drawbar pulled out only, the following notes, starting with the low F, closely agree with the frquencies specified.

F5 697 Hz.
A6 880 Hz.
C#6 1108 Hz.
E6 1318 Hz.
F#6 1479 Hz.
G#6 1661 Hz.
E7 2637 Hz.

A better idea is, of course, to use an accurate signal generator. If the generator is off, you can calibrate it by using A= 880 Hz. Or, Ma Bell herself can help you. A touch tone phone operates very accurately with each row and column having a single frequency. To get 697 Hz, simply press any two buttons on the top row.

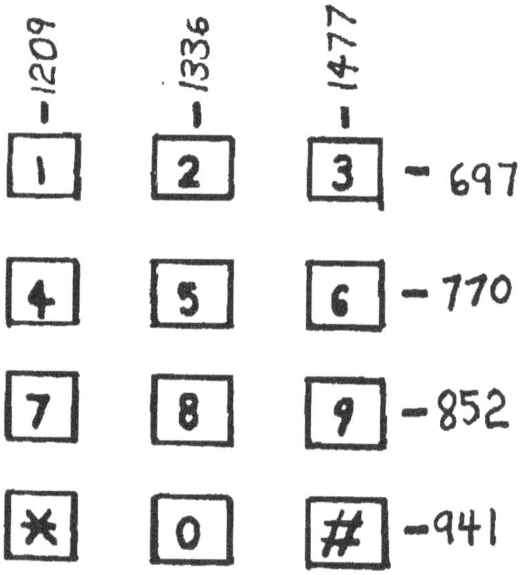

```
     1209   1336   1477
      |      |      |
    [ 1 ]  [ 2 ]  [ 3 ] - 697

    [ 4 ]  [ 5 ]  [ 6 ] - 770

    [ 7 ]  [ 8 ]  [ 9 ] - 852

    [ * ]  [ 0 ]  [ # ] - 941
```

To tune a signal generator with a touch-tone phone, connect the generator output to the two microphone terminals in the phone handset, press 1 and 2, and tune generator until "beats" stop. Generator is now putting out 697.

Several YIPLs have written us that the original oscillator schematic has unnecessary parts for temperature stability. We have found that best results necessitate these parts because pay phones are often in cold parts, and one would not want to call a friend long distance just to play him an out-of-tune organ, now would we?

Published for informational purposes only by Youth Hot Line Reports, Inc.

For those of you who are interested in obtaining the original information on boxing, the Bell System Technical Journal, in 1960 or in 1961, put out an article called Multifrequency signaling systems. You might find it in an engineering library, if Bell doesn't find it first. We would appreciate it if an astute YiPPler would go there armed with a razor blade, and after liberating the article, send it to us for publication. We will return it to her/him.

A subscription to YIPL costs $4/yr. if you got.
TAP Room 418, 152 W. 42 St., N.Y., N.Y. 10036

7

Blue Box Fans! Want a groovy new way to send your beeps into the pay phone downstairs, with lower distortion, and less risk of being overheard? An induction coupler, Model PC-48,$9.95 each, is available from Trinetics,Inc. 807 W. 3rd St.,Mishawaka, In. 46544. It slips over the ear-piece(that's right) and can also pick up conversations for taping. But keep at least a speaker jack on your box for tuning, because tuning a box over a phone line, even on a local phone call, is definitely not cool.

Credit for the Credit Card Code ticle inside must be given to you readers, and to the news-papers around the country that are risking their neck printing it up, we say thanx. Which again proves if we contribute to each other, we all benefit.

Keep sending in suggestions for the following:
Corporation ripoffs, establish-ment fucks, healthful hints, names and addresses of our friends who wish to be known, new ser-vices, new outrages,new devices and plans for them.
You're having trouble with find-ing #14 Brass washers(dime-size) and we know about it. Some stores have them listed as 1/4" I.D., or as 11/16" O.D. washers. Some will refuse to sell to freaks, so have your respectable-looking friends go in and play plumber, or call in orders and then play messenger.
Send us results, and all of you do a study on where they work, what machines require tape over the hole and stuff like that. We're compiling material for an article on using, making and living on slugs. Get with it!

LETTERS (CONTINUED ON NEXT PAGE)

Dear YIPL,
Here's a suggestion for YIPL readers: One very good way to obtain extra phones is to get them out of empty apartments from non-phreek friends who have had their phones disconnected but not removed. Here in Gainesville Ma Bell doesn't remove phones from empty apartments until new tenants move in and order their own phones. The servicemen simply take what's there, and if its not there it doesn't matter because Ma Bell doesn't keep good records in Gainesville and probably most other collegetowns where people are moving all the time. G.P.,Gainesville, Fla.

Dear YIPL,
......LOVERS LETTER is a monthly public-ation offering practical, realistic advice for men on the art of love. LOVERS LETTER tells where to find girls, how to approach them and how to make them like you. We also give frank advice on how to extablish satisfying love/sex relationships. A sub-scription is $10/yr. LL publishing Co., Box 5834-H, Bethesda,Md. 20014.
-YIPL readers- We checked this out and if its in your pipe it ain't too bad. If you want, free further details are available on how to sell subscriptions.

IMPORTANT NOTICE
There is a credit card system used by the phone company called the Code Billing sys-tem. A sample number is 014-5742-019. The first number must be 0 or 1,and the last three numbers must be between 001-499.Say to the operator "Code billing operator.My number is ....If they ask what company it is, make one up,.or hang up. Of course, call from a booth. This is under test now, so let us know what happens.,.........

Y.I.P.L.:
Rip offs that what you are, I send
you a check,you cashed it and never
send me anything.
I hate getting rip off by anyone,
and I'm going to do all that I can
to let the people know what you are.
This is the fourth letter that I
haved send you, you had haved more
that enough time to fix everything.
Well this the last letter that I will
send you, and I hope you enjoy all your
going to get.Rip off! R.N.,Bronx,N.Y.

Friends:
I'm a high school student in N.J. and
one day last week they herded us all
into the auditorium were this very
straight dude from N.J. Bell proceed-
ed to give us a speech about all the
wonderful things we have to thank them
for(Better living thru Ma Bell). The
only reason I can see for this propog-
anda is that they realized how bad kids
are fucking them and they have decided
to nip this conspiracy in the bud. But
the real reason I wrote this is that I
went up to the stage and asked this robot
to say a few words about a real scientific
advancement, the blue box. He said that he
didn't want to hear it and started to walk
away so I started to tell people about it.
This got him very uptight and he came back
and told everyone that the blue box would
soon be obsolete because Ma Bell was planning to vary the tone frequencies from
area to area and make it impossible to
break out of the area. I don't really
understand this but I thought I'd tell you
to see if it is bullshit or not because
those fuckers have me worried that the toy
organ I'm building will soon be of limited
usefulness.Yours truly a hopelessly para-
noid reader.
-Our opinion of this statement by N.J.Bell
is that to vary tone frequencies will cost
an incredible amount, require that all employees be back at work to make the change,
would necessitate changing every single
multifrequency sender in the country. In
other words, it's possible, but to try to
do it without raising rates and spending
time, possibly years, is not. So build your
organ and the fact that you will no longer
contribute to their treasury will serve to
prolong the changeover.-Ed.

Dear Yip-Line-
I just tried to make a long distance
call from a public telephone to order
Mexican 10 centavo pieces-which work
in pay phones a quarters. I was just
about to dial the number and insert the
few 10 centavo pieces I had left when I
noticed that the dial had been ripped
off. I have not commented on public
issues in a long time but I believe
that people who rip dials off pay
phones are hurting their brothers
and sisters more than the telephone
company. Alexander Graham Bell
Dear Y.I.P.L.,
If any of you out there still eat meat,
here's a helpful hint on getting the
best and/or the biggest piece for the
cheapest price possible. Everyone knows
we can't shoplift or steal-the price
we pay is too large if you're caught.
So just take the best piece of meat and
the cheapest piece, carefully peel the
price label off the cheaper one and stick
it on the good one. Return the one you
don't want, and smile sweetly at th :ash
lady as the stuff goes through. Fuck the
establishment-I love you Y.1.P.L. K&B,
Florida.

Dear YIPL-
Here's 3 bucks-all we can afford now but
enough to ask you to please start sending
our issues in covered envelopes; we're
getting a few hassles unnecessarily(small
town-P.O. workers are buddies to cops,
etc.) and we hope a few dollars for you
will help.Power to the pcople. L&W

From Chicago Tribune, Feb. 2,'72

He Had Their Number

A Los Angeles man who figured out how to tap himself
into Pacific Telephone Company's computer by using his
push button phone was arrested Tuesday for stealing more
than $1 million worth of the company's equipment. Police
said Jerry N. Schneider, 21, had been ordering the ~~~
puter to have equipment sent to a company warehouse t
he had acquired keys, and he picked it up in the early mor-
ing hours before warehousemen arrived. The gambit became so successful, police said, that Schneider started his
own business selling telephone equipment, and had hired 10
employes to help him.

1972 CREDIT CARD CODE

PREFIX

EXAMPLE - 777-3311 021 Q (ITT, NEW YORK CITY)

The New 1972 Credit Card Code is the same old shit. However, instead of the 6th digit being used to determine the code letter, it is now the 4th. And the ten code letters are different. Take note and pass the word along to friends, university billboards, local newspapers, and as extra items on your schools announcements. This is, of course, to discourage any degenerates who would attempt to rip off Ma Bell. They will realize that when they do it, everybody will be doing it, and it won't be fun.

1 - Z	ATLANTA - 035	MIAMI - 044
2 - J		MINN. - 126
3 - Q	BERKELY - 167	NORTH N·J. - 091, 094
4 - S	BOSTON - 001	NEW MEXICO - 105
5 - D		
6 - H	CHICAGO - 097	NEW YORK CITY - 072,074,
7 - U	CLEVELAND - 082	(+ VICINITY) 021
	CONN. - 020	
8 - M	DETROIT - 096,083	PHILA. - 041
9 - A		PITTS. - 030
0 - X - 064	HOUSTON - 151	SAN. FRAN. - 158
SO.N - 064 SALT LAKE CITY 015	LOS ANGELES - 182	WASH. D.C. - 032

TIPS: At night (5pm to Mid.) the majority of the pig operators are working and your chances of running into one is greater. Avoid peak calling periods. They might question you and stuff like that, in which case hang up, or if asked the number calling, say that its a phone booth(which it should be). Don't continually use the same phone booth, or the same credit card number, or call at the same time or same day. It's easy to vary your schedule. Known phony credit card numbers are kept on a PHONY LIST, so keep changing the number, gang.

If you call in the Atlanta area, the operators there have a list of all possible telephone prefixes for that area. A credit card number having a 035 along with a prefix that is non-existant in Atlanta is obviously phony. Make sure your prefix in the number exists in the area of your code.

Just because you get your call through, don't think your done. The operator may come on the line silently to verify the call, or she may simply stay on for a few seconds to see that you got through. If you gave her a rubber number and she knows it, she may let the call go through just so her supervisor can get on the line to invade your privacy, tape record the conversation, trace your calling number, and later bust you. So don't say right out to your friend,"Hey, man, I just used a phoney credit card number".

If you call someone, make sure they know what to tell them when and if they contact him/her about the call. Have your friend say"I'm sorry operator but many people use this phone, and I get so many calls its hard to remember, but I think his first name was Steve, and he called from Cincinnati." (They already know the city, so you aren't helping them but sound sincere).

Never give a last name, or his phone number. Be real polite, if they are. But refuse to pay if they bill you. Note your phony calls down so you can see if they pull something like that. Refusing to pay leaves you in very good shape of ending up paying. And by the way, they might look through old phone bills to see who called in the past, and they might say that so-and-so called you and you should admit it. Well, DON'T ADMIT IT. They're only guessing. If they knew they wouldn't bother calling you, now would they?

For those of you who can't take it any longer and are planning on moving to Canada, you might be interested to know that there are a goodly number of YIPLs there already. You might also want to get a copy of The Canadian Whole Earth Almanac, 341 Bloor St. West, Room 208, Toronto, Canada for the sum of $3, or a years subscription for $9. Community Television work is being done in Canada by Videotech, 111 Sparks St., Ottawa, Ontario. Write them.

Various readers have been suggesting that we discover a way to let phone phreeks contact each other. To some, printing names and phone numbers is not too cool. However, to some, receiving YIPL is not too cool. We want to hear more from you as to suggestions for ways to do it, or if you think we should just print a list of people who want to be printed.
When writing to us, never place the stamp 1&1/2 inches too low or it won't be postmarked. We can't do that. Why, just think what that would mean. The post office would lose income, and we would no longer be able to afford to build bombs and defoliants and RAID. Not only that, but our elder statesmen would start to make statements to the press about yippies and ripper-offers. Furthermore, the post office would be forced to stop using the dumb machines to postmark letters and to handcancel instead, thus forcing the hiring of twelve million workers and ending unemployment in this country, which would in turn cut down profits to the nice folks who brought you Attica and Hiroshima. No, we can't have that happen. So be good little automatons and put the stamp right up in the corner there, where Robby the Robot and his pal Dicky can put their good seal of approval on it.

We'll be back sometime in the near future with an article you will find well worth waiting for, we hope. Till then.....A subscription to YIPLis $2/yr, and back issues are 50¢ each. We will give you a free subscription if you really cannot afford it, and that's why we cost what we do. If you can afford it, send us bread and stamps, please. YIPL, Room 504, 152 W. 42 St., N.Y.,N.Y. 10036, and don't send cash!

#1-Installing extensions #2-Blue Box Story #3-Telecommand Story
#4-Pay Phone issue #5-Organ plans(1) #6-Organ plans(2) #7-Tuning Organ

Published for informational purposes only by Youth Hot Line Reports, Inc.

Address all mail and checks to :

TAP, 152 W. 42 ST, ROOM 418, NY 10036

8

"Help! Help! I'm out of order!"

YĪPL

NUMBER 9
MARCH-APRIL '72

Instead of being the period of good will to men on Wednesday morning our citizens were somewhat excited on learning that a resident of Main St. had cut all the telephone wires that passed over his house, thus cutting off the residents of the lower portion of the Town from its service.

We've got something rather special this month(or months) and you can find it inside. This article has, to our knowledge, never been published with details for use. It is so good, that it is not worth our getting hassled for printing it if you readers don't support our action by reprinting it and giving it out. Here's how to do this and make it effective; Mail it to people and places far away from you as well as in your own community. Have a stock of Xeroxed copies so when you pick up yippies hitching you can lay them onto it, and they will then spread the news. Papers should print it, and radio station people should tell listeners to rite to them for a copy. In the ..ext letter you write to anyone you know, include a copy of this article. We are really pushing this for several reasons, but mostly because it can seriosly affect Ma Bells profits and therefore policy if it goes into widespread use, & it should. It is wrong to assume that they can easily change the system and render the device ineffective, because it would take much time wherever they did it, & it would have to be done by people, who need the work anyway. Build them and sell them, but not for more than five bucks. The parts are cheap,maybe two dollars. GET GOING!

BUGS...

For those of you interested in an article on bugging and debugging devices, see Radio-Electronics, February 1972. We are forced to ?fer you to it because of lack of space here.

Our back issue department has a headache, so we're changing things a bit. We're combing thru the issues and putting together feature sheets on the major articles that appear. So far, they are as follows:

Credit card calls and helpful hints, Pay phone hints, Installing phones

This will speed our now sluggish back issue service, while insuring that you receive revisions and full information on past articles. Price is 25¢ each but send enough to make up for people who can't afford them (like us). When you get the shit, be sure to duplicate it immediately before it becomes all wrinkled, then start passing it out. You'll meet all kinds of far out people that way and it's been proven that passing out YIPLs reduces the chance of heart attack, (for you but not for Rockefeller).

Friends,freaks, and pigs;
Of late, I have been receiving fewer computer cards to return with my bills but my friendly Public Service Co.s and good 'ol Ma Bell persist in them. It seems to me that I once read of a local freak who not only cracked the code, but also went so far as to use it to his advantage. I feel it would be a great contribution to the cause of all of us if you were to encourage your readers to send in what they know so that you might publish it.-A key punch person.

For those of you who want to know how to tell if your phone is tapped, give up. Best way to tell is by flipping a coin. Clicks mean nothing but poor service usually, and silence is often more dangerous. Don't talk on the phone!

dear yipl; you should know that the check I'm sending cost nothing to write. No charges for printing checks, deposits, writing checks, monthly statements. Just watch the overdrafts and postdated checks-they cost $3 each. Write for account information to UNB,461 Forbes, Pittsburgh, Pa. 15213(that's The Union National Bank of Pittsburgh). -Your friend in New York.

Dear YIPL;
If any phreaks would like to visit Atlanta this way there is a pay phone on the strip near Roy Rogers drive Inn(876-9639area code 404). Its busy a lot, but if you call a dope dealing freak will probably answer. A good phone is at the U of Ga. at Atlanta. 404-543-9224. Call a student and turn him on tb the credit card code! Skinny Bobby Harper, a very cool D.J. at WIIN would like to hear from phone phreaks. Call him and talk on the air 6 am. -9 am.Mon. thru Fri., 6am.-10 am. Sat. 404-892-3777. Relate the credit card code to his listeners.
I just had quite a good night of phreaking. After some of the best Mexican I ever had I called info in Houston. The operator was real nice. She answered my questions with "surely" and I told her that the operators in N.Y. said that too & it was just a catchy phrase that them yankees were into. She said it was in the operator's manual and I told her she sounded like a very nice girl and I was sorry that the establishment had made a robot out of her. Then she admitted to what's in the guts of every true american. She hates the phone co. Dig it!
  I believe that if you have the right tension bar and pick you can open up the cash box on a pay phone. See what YIPL readers can find out about this. Does opening the lock trigger an alarm in the phone co?
  Drop a dime or a washer in one of the old coke machines(red and short) and press the handle down all the way and get your soda, then lift up half way and press down again and out comes another coke. The whole fucking machine can be emptied for a washer or a filed-down penny.
  The Cheif of Security of Southern Bell here is Gerald E. McDaniels and he seems to like to talk to phone freaks. So why don't some of you people call him and tell him you're calling from ____ with a phoney card and/or a box.His office is 404-529-6036. He's in and out all day chasing phreaks so call him at home. Dial 404 963-1640. He's kind of hard to catch so we advise calling between 2 and 3 am.Ask him how he's going to catch him and tell him he's full of shit. Your nameless comrade.

To:YIPL
Thought you might be interested in the current issue of Advertising Age. It's about poor Mr. Gerrity of ITT, who is in charge of the company's 93-MILLION DOLLAR A YEAR advertising program. If this wasn't enough, some people are saying some very unkind things about his giving $400,000 in a bribe to the Justice Department. In case any of you would like to console Mr. Gerrity in this time of crisis, he can be reached c/o ITT,320 Park Ave.,N.Y.,N.Y. or telephone: 212-PL 2 6000.
  Keep up the good work!
-W.,New York,N.Y.
Ed. note-I urge Yipls to take advant-age of this opportunity to show how concerned we are with current events.

Boycott the War!

SUPER-DUPER PROJECT!

This article will describe to you how to receive long distance calls at no charge to the caller. The device is simple to build and use, and it is less dangerous than all other long distance methods with the exception, perhaps, of credit cards.

The phone company tells you are on the phone when you are drawing direct current. This device uses a resistor to reduce the dc, and a capacitor to ensure that the voice sounds will not be also reduced. The part values are not critical. Simply break one of the two wires (green or red) going to the phone and install the unit. Extensions cannot be used also when using this device on a call, because when an extension is picked up the dc starts to flow again, and the billing starts.

To use: Know when a friend is calling long distance. Normally the unit should be left on "normal", but when the call comes in, you must pick up the phone and then flip the switch to "free" within half a second. This short period of time that the phone is answered normally stops the ringing, and should be performed during a ring cycle. It sounds a lot harder than it is, because if you wait too long between pick-up and switching to "free" then the call will be disconnected, but you have to wait at least a second to do that. If you don't wait long enough, or accidentally flip switch before picking up, the ring will be heard in the earpiece along with your friend, so hang up and do it agin! It'll keep ringing until you do it the right way.

On local calls, if you answer with the above procedure, you will be cut off within a short time. As always, have friends call at varying times,& never stay on more than 15 minutes. The device is only for incoming calls to a home phone, and the caller must call direct, without an operator.

This device is so good, and so cheap, that you will probably want to Xerox this article to pass out at demonstations, riots, colleges, post on bulletin boards, send to all the underground newspapers you know of. Do it today!

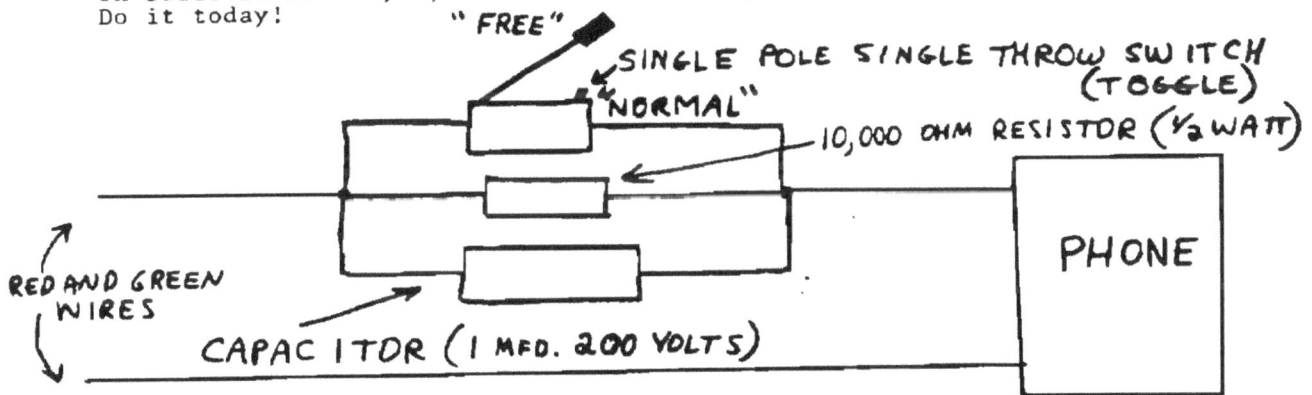

RECYCLE THIS ARTICLE! TAP, ROOM 418, 152 W. 42. ST, N.Y.,NY. 10036

See issue #11 for simpler plans!

For those of us who live in New York City, a real treat may be had by visiting the new telephone building being built on Church Street below Canal. This building is described by some as the most incredibly arrogant piece of architecture they have ever seen. It's described by others as a monolith. It's huge, and is of solid something, but it looks like concrete. There are no windows, as in the blockhouses at Cape Kennedy. There are just these 4 huge openings about halfway up for some unknown purpose. If Hitler had had enough money and time, he would have wanted one of these battle stations for his very own. It appears capable of withstanding atomic attack, if that means anything, because if anyone were to use an atomic device, it would be our government or the phone company itself, and probably on us. Oh well, go on down and have a look at things to come.

The telephone company offers its operators two kinds of headsets to wear on their heads for 8 hours a day. One kind is made of a very hard plastic and chafes and presses into the ear and side of the head. This is the standard. The other kind has a comfortable ear mount which is cushioned and much more desirable. Would you believe that you have to pay them for this type of headset if you are an operator? The phone company, after all, has to do something to make back all that money squandered on operator's outrageous salaries. Like even start charging for information calls, as they will soon be doing in many places. When that happens, we will urge people to strike phone service, phone employees to strike, and people to stop paying their extortion notices, and it looks like we should be getting ready. See y'all in San Diego.

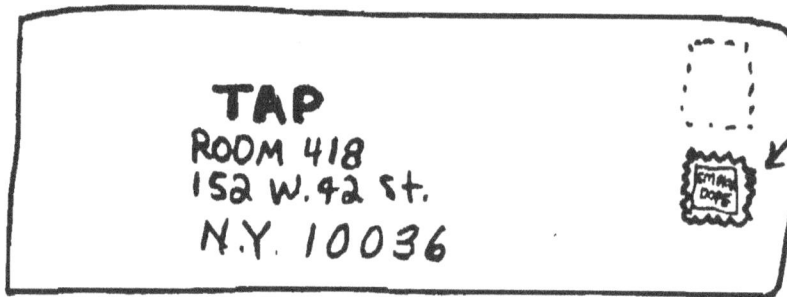

TAP
ROOM 418
152 W. 42 St.
N.Y. 10036

LOWERING STAMP 1½ INCHES AVOIDS POSTMARK, OR COVER WITH ELMER'S GLUE (SEE #39)

HAVE ALL YOUR FRIENDS JOIN YIPL! $4/YR. DON'T SEND CASH!
Make checks payable to TAP

Published for informational purposes only by the Technological American Party (TAP).

9

REPORT THE PERVERT WHO GIVES YOU THIS, KIDS!

YIPL
NUMBER 10
MAY, 1972

BE SURE TO WRITE TO:
Vocations for Social Change
Box 13,Canyon,Ca. 94516
          and
New England Free Press
791 Tremont St.,Boston,Ma. 02118
Ask them for free bibliography.
Write to them today before you forget.

READ THIS

The Boston Peoples Yellow Pages is
#1 and well worth it. Write to dem
at 351 Broadway, Cambridge,Ma.
02139. Or write to People Yellow
Pages at Emmaus House, 241 E. 116
St.,NY,NY 10029. It's free but they
need contributions to stay alive
so help them out,OK?

   While you're doing that, you'll
want to have a PYP in your own community if you don't already. Write
to the above about forming one, or
just do it, or if one is forming,
help. But make sure to publicise
YIPL and some of our articles in
it, and write us if you need pub-
licity or our back issues.

   There are so many radio stations
and papers in your community that
need feature articles on things
like YIPL that it isn't funny. Go
to these places and tell them
you'll prepare a show on phone
politics and technology. If you
receive this, you are hereby autho-
rized to represent YIPL in your
community and should start doing
so immediately. Its absolutely
legal, but that shouldn't stop you.

START YOUR OWN LOCAL CHAPTER OF YIP!

IF YOU ARE ABLE TO CONTACT OR WORK WITH HEALTH
CLINICS, FOOD COOPS, LIBRARIES, HEADSHOPS, DAY CARE
CENTERS, COLLECTIVES, RADIO STATIONS, NEWPAPERS,
BOOKSTORES, PUBLICATIONS, OR ANY COMMUNICATIONS MEDIUM
THAT REACHES MANY PEOPLE, OR EVEN JUST YOUR OWN
COMMUNITY, YOU CAN BEGIN ORGANIZING INFORMATION DRIVES.
SOME IDEAS ARE NEWSLETTERS, FREE SCHOOL CLINICS &
TEACH-INS ON PHONES AND PHONE COMPANY PRACTICES, INFO-
RMATION TABLES, DEMONSTRATIONS, COMMUNITY EDUCATION
MEETINGS ON PHONES, ETC. START THINKING OF OTHER IDEAS
AND LET US KNOW. WE CAN ORGANIZE GUEST SPEAKERS ON
YIPL + SOME YIPL READERS WILL VOLUNTEER TO BE PART
OF PHONE COMPANY TEACH-INS. WRITE TO US SOON!!!

Dear YIPL,
Here's a toll free loop around no. in Miami. 821 9005 or 821 9006(often busy). You can get free local service by calling the operator and saying "Operator I just lost my dime in the fucking phone" and she'll either give a free call or she'll send you a dime in the mail. By the way, always call the operator after a pay phone call and ask her to refund the 45¢ you lost before you found out the phone was busted(the one across the street) or when at home, after you made a cheap call,call the operator and say you didn't get through but got a recording instead and you want credit for the call. Many Bell offices accept collect calls, as do some pig corporations.

Sunday I tried to call London and the overseas operator got suspicious and put a recorder on the line so I hung up the phone and ran across the street and a pig car came within 30 seconds. Whew! I didn't know you could get a pig that fast even if you called for one. Tell everyone about being careful with overseas operators! Keep on dialing.M.F. Somewhere,U.S.A.

Dear YIPL,
I have located a supplier for No. 14 brass washers and some info concerning them. Most hardware stores will not carry them for brass is too expensive. If you get them at a store don't ask for No. 14 or they might not know what you're talking about. Ask for 11/16 outside diameter,with 1/4 inch inside diameter. Your best,cheapest supplier will be an industrial mill supply house. Look 'em up in the yellow pages under mill supply or electrical supply. Ask for #14 L Brass flat washers. Pay cash,convince them to sell to you wholesale, and don't sign any sales slips! Love and Struggle, C.R.,Louisville,Ky

For SALE- We are selling T-shirts sten-
ciled with a big red fist to raise money for our local high school underground in Louisville. Send $1.50 to:T-shirt Deal, c/o Charlie Rosenberg,3718 Rouge Way, Louisville,Ky. 40218 Thanks a lot folks.

Dear YIP Line people,
We urge you to organize with us a massive telephone campaign in your home community aimed at reaching as many households and businesses as possible. We suggest using the following method to once again make the war a public issue. Our major method will be a phone calling campaign consisting simply of the following: "Hello,I called to ask you to think about whether Nixon lied about ending the war. Thank you." We believe that putting the message in the form of a non-rhetorical question is both more thought provoking and less alienating. This campaign will include newpaper ads and media involvement carrying the simple message;That Nixon lied about ending the war. Please join us. "The Nixon Lied Campaign" 424 North Aurora St.,Ithaca,N.Y. 14850

Dear Friends,
It has come to my attention that Bell Tel has developed a device similar to the Telecommand except that it does not have to be installed in your phone. It can be connected to the main box in the basement of an apartment building or on a telephone pole for a house job. To defeat this infernal device, you can use a S.P.S.T. switch to turn off the speaker and mouthpiece yet allow calls to come through. From the phone handset, the red and the white wire both go to the same terminal on the phone block. Make them both go thru a switch when you want to be sure the Telecommand isn't being used.
-The Old Wazoo

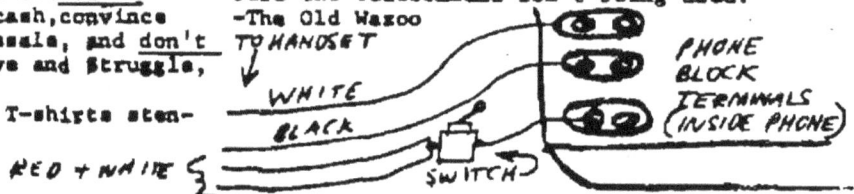

TO HANDSET
WHITE
BLACK
RED + WHITE
SWITCH
PHONE BLOCK TERMINALS (INSIDE PHONE)

Here's a little trick I picked up & I'm letting you know in case there is a need to stop traffic in L.A. The signal boxes on corners of streets that control & regulate the lights can be opened by a sharp blow with ones fist on the side of the box even level with the keyhole. Now the door will swing open and one can control or stop or freeze the signal. Can be useful if you're in a hurry.

OTHER PIG LINES TO TIE UP DAILY:
Avis(ITT)-800 621 8430 (Area 312)
Sheraton Hotels-800 -325 3535
TWA- 800 621 6640 (Area 312)
Holiday Inn-800 621 5511(Area 312)

For other areas,call 800 555 1212 for Watts Information. Remember, it's all FREE!

When writing to YIPL, always place stamp envelope. Most of our mail comes this w

A load of people have been writing us that our Super-Duper Project is defunct when they try to make it work. They also have been saying that the circuit on page 78 of <u>Steal This Book</u> is better or its worse or what the hell is it etc. Let's clear up the mystery.

The aforementioned circuit in <u>Steal</u> can be used to receive free incoming calls. However, we have tried both and prefer ours for the following reasons:

1-The huge capacitor is hard to fit inside a phone. A large number of MFD.'s is necessary in that circuit, and since 90 volts comes down your line each ring, 200 working volts is needed to prevent destruction of the capacitor. 100 MFD. at 200 volts is a big fucker. The large number of Mfd.'s is used to essentially "pick-up" your phone for an instant, as must be done manually in our unit. This pickup stops the ringing but is not long enough to start the billing. That's the whole secret to Bell's billing equiptment. Their newest system is foolproof but hardly in use anywhere. You know if your area has the unbeatable system if your dial tone comes on immediately upon lifting switchook, rather that 1/2 second later, but most areas have the delay.

If you have tried a unit and it disconnects your call a few seconds after you answer on "Free", try to make the operation of answering as fast as possible. That is, pick up the phone on normal and <u>as fast as you can</u> switch to "Free". If you don't give it at least 1/10 second it will probably continue to ring, so try giving it a little more, and so on. By picking up on "Normal" and waiting more than 1/2 second or so and then switching to "Free" you essentially pick up and then hang up, so you get disconnected in a few seconds.

2- The large capacitor in the <u>Steal</u> circuit can cause sparks, hence the 10 ohm resistor across the switch. You might get a shock.

3-When you pick up on "Free" in the <u>Steal</u> circuit it automatically answers it, immediately. In our circuit picking up on "Free" will allow you to hear the caller, who may have been told in advance to be talking while it rings so you can hear him and know to answer Free, by then hanging up, flipping switch to normal and then-Lift and Flip as usual. This can avoid embarrasing moments when a friend calls with an operator on the line who might get suspicious. Try to only answer with "Free" method when you know who's calling, but if you can't then prearrange with friends to talk or sing into phone during first few rings to tip you off.

That's why we published ours. By the way, both lines will let you listen to your line without "picking up" your phone. Just flip to "free" and listen to your empty line. Hear repairmen and repairwomen placing taps and talking to each other while they do it. Flip to "Normal" and hear the dial tone come on, as the phone equiptment thinks you've just picked up. It's fun!

The capacitor can alert the phone co. if its too big, too. No bigger than 1 Mfd.,please, and be sure the unit has no + or - on it; most don't.

See Issue 11 for a simple version of the Super-Duper Projec

The Computer Says No

NEW YORK POST, FRIDAY, MARCH 24, 1972

1&1/2 inches lower than normal on y. and saves us a lot in postage.

BACK ISSUES
Back issues are 50¢ each, and the following are available.
Blue Box information and story plus tuning hints.
Credit card calls and how not to get caught.
Pay Phone Issue.
Super-Duper Project(Free incoming calls).

To those working on other circuits for public use, we urge you to send them
in to us for publication when fully tested. We will be publishing other
interesting ideas for projects from time to time. Thanks to all those who
write letters and circuits. Even if they're not used, we test those we can
and condense the information to pass it along to you readers.
    We still need information slugs and machines and which ones do and don't
work and how to make them work. Do some experimenting around and let us
know.
    YIPL does not publish these incredibly great and useful pieces of info
in order to see them put to use. We publish simply so that people can sit
back and stare at interesting electronic circuits,which have been known to
have a soothing effect upon baby rats and presumably humans, too.

COMMUNITAS- A new community journal for those interested in coming together
with others while retaining a degree of activity with the rest of the world.
You can get a sample copy free, so it can't be too bad. Subscription-$6 for
6 issues.Communitas,121 W. Center College St.,Yellow Springs,Ohio 45387

Published for informational purposes only by the Youth International Party Line.

Nab Students While Building Phone System

Two MIT students, whom
police said were setting up
their own telephone system,
were arrested yesterday because of an open manhole.
    Julian West, 18, of 518
Beacon st., Back Bay, an
MIT dormitory, and Kevin P.
Koch, 19, of Ames st., Cambridge, had their cases continued to May 3 by Roxbury
District Court Judge Elwood
McKenney.
    Sgt. Matthew Loughlin and
Patrolmen Albert Bozzi and
Robert Vasselian found a
manhole cover out of place
in front of the Beacon st.
dorm.
    They seized one of the
youths outside the manhole
and the other inside where
they said a miniature switchboard had been set up.
    The youths were charged
with injuring lines of the Boston Edison Co. A communications hookup with a dormitory across the street was in
progress, police said.

SUBSCRIBE NOW! $2 (IF YOU GOT IT)

Dear Customer:
Texaco is Working to Keep Your Trust.
As part of our Travel Card Service,
we tried to call you recently to
thank you personally for buying Texaco. You are a valued customer, and
we are anxious to acquaint you with
all of the many services offered
through our Texaco Travel Card Sales
Program. Since we could not reach
you, we invite you to call us at the
Toll Free number-800-392-4963 from
7:30-4:15 P.M. Central Standard Time
Mon-Fri. We look forward to hearing
from you, and Thanks Again for buying
Texaco.

FROM:
YIPL, ROOM 504, 152 W. 42 ST., N.Y., N.Y. 10036

TO:

SPECIAL CONVENTION ISSUE!

YOUTH INTERNATIONAL PARTY LINE
NO. 11

HI! I'M TELLY. FLY ME TO MIAMI!

JUNE-JULY 1972

LETTERS

The World's First Phone Phreak Convention is being held on July 11-15, in Miami Beach! The Celebration of Change will include, in addition, teach-ins on telephones, contests, meetings with nationally-known phone phreaks. Plus the unveiling of new devices never yet revealed. Courses are going to be held on Phone Politics, Phone ripoffs, establishment ripoffs, and peoples technology.
If you want to help or teach a class, write us immediately and include your phone no.
At the same time there will be other events too, such as antiwar demos, women's rights, health care, anti-smack information and actions, and many other happenings. Get in touch with YIP in Miami for these if you want to be involved.
The Convention and the Celebration of Change will be an incredible learning scene and you should start telling everyone you know to be there. If you are a budding phone phreak, you'll learn how a phone works, and how to make it work for you. Or come down for the pot parade to legalize Marijuana, but COME DOWN, AND BRING YOUR FRIENDS. Put signs in freak stores and post notices in schools-MIAMI BEACH-JULY 11-15. There'll be food, sun and fun.

Gentlemen:
I am including the name of the Company that can provide those interested with all types of telephone devices as well as info. They also have two correspondence courses that I believe are the best (only) of their kind. One is a telephone engineering course-how to make your own clandestine devices. The second is a "spy" course. You & your readers will flip over their catalog. Cost is $1 deductable from any purchase-and well worth it.
Don Britton Enterprise, P.O. Drawer G, Waikiki, Hawaii 96815. -G.B.
Readers have written for info on the Peoples Yellow Pages. We're making a list of the PYP's all over the country, so if you know one in your area, send us the address and whether or not they're doing more of the same.
New York PYP is at N.Y. Switchboard, 134 w. 4 St., NYC 10012.
For more on telephone groups working for changing the Bell System, the Source Catalog #1 has many groups listed, such as Womens groups, U.S. Govt. inspecting phones, Grass Roots, etc. Write to Source at Box 21066, Washington, D.C. 20009.

WRITE TO:
YIP, ROOM 201, 1674 MERIDIAN AVE, MIAMI BEACH
PHONE 305-531-8845

RECEIVE FREE LONG-DISTANCE CALLS!

Now you can receive calls at no charge to the caller, and anyone, even a child, can convert their phone to do this in less than 30 minutes. You only need two parts: A "single pole, single throw toggle switch" and a "10,000 ohm, 1/2 watt, 10% resistor". Hardware stores carry switches with two wires already on them, and these are convenient to use. The resistor can be bought for 20¢ at a radio-tv supply or electronic hobbyist store, such as Lafayette Radio. If you can't find a switch with wires already on it, get one with screw terminals so you can easily attacn on wires.

Cut two pieces of wire at least 6 inches long. Strip off the insulation 1/2 inch from each end. Attach one wire to each of the two switch screws, and you now have a switch with two 6 inch wires connected.

Turn your normal dial phone upside down and unscrew the two screws, and remove the case. You will now see a small metal box with 16 screws on top and wires connected to them. Locate the screw marked "F" using our diagram and loosen it. Wrap one of the resistor wires around it and tighten the screw. Loosen the "RR" screw and remove the green wire. Then wrap the other resistor wire around the "RR" screw along with one of the switch wires. Tighten the "RR" screw and be sure the wires only touch the proper terminals and no others. Finally, wrap the remaining switch wire around the green wire you just removed and wrap the two up tightly in scotch or electrical tape.

Close up the phone, running the switch wires out the side or rear of the case. Hang up receiver and get a piece of tape and a pen. Pick up the phone and flip switch to the position that gives you a dial tone. Using tape, mark this position of the switch "Normal". Now flip the switch to the other position and the dial tone should stop. Mark this position of the switch "Free". If you don't get it to work right, check your wiring for a break or a wire touching a nearby screw inside the phone.

Leave the switch "Normal" for everyday use. When your friends call, quic y lift and drop receiver as fast as you can. This is very important that you do it quickly. This should stop the rings. If not, do it again. Then switch to "Free", pick up the phone and talk. Keep all calls as short as you can, always less than 15 minutes. At end of call, hang up, then switch to "Normal". If the call is local, switch to "Normal" immediately or you may be cut off. Your friend can call right back, so the shorter the call the better it is.

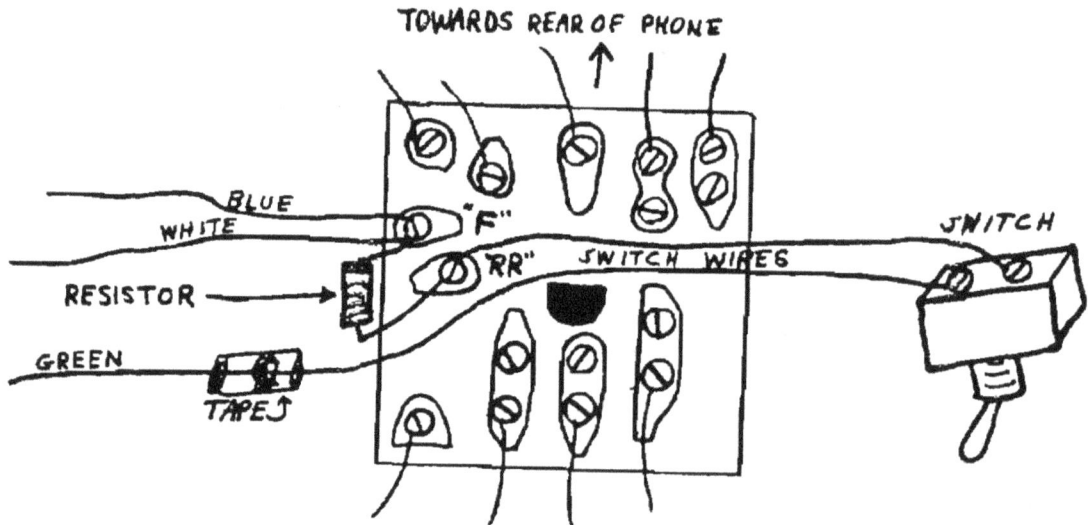

HOW IT WORKS

When you call someone long distance, you are billed from the moment they answer. The phone company knows you answer when a certain amount of electric current flows through the phone. However, the resistor cuts down the amount of current below the point of billing,yet lets enough go by to operate the mouthpiece. Inside the phone, connected across the F and RR terminals, is a capacitor, a device which allows more volume for your voice without using any more electric current.

Answering the phone normally for a fraction of a second stops the rings, but does not let enough current flow to start the billing. If you answer normally for even one full second, however, billing will start. Therefore, hanging up and switching to free will cut you off.

To render the device ineffective, the phone company would have to spend billions of dollars and many years of changing the country's phone systems. Using this device is illegal in some places, and we strongly urge you to inspect all phones you see for the device. If you see it, rip it out and eat it immediately.

By the way, you cannot use an extension phone during a free call unless it too is modified and the switch is in "Free".

YIPL is $2 for a year's issues, if you can afford it. If you can, send stamps or bread to pay for those who can't, & turn someone on to YIPL today!

TECHNICAL DATA 25¢ EACH
- BLUE BOX INFO + TUNING
- CREDIT CARD CALLS

This article is essentially the same as published in Ramparts, who has been suppressed by the Phone Company. Ramparts has taken apart the State Dept.,the Defense Dept. and the whole fucking government and no hassles but the article about the phone company and POW! Which is why YIPL exists, to get the vital information to the people if there's no other way to get it to them. You supply the information, and you get more back. Send us ideas, tell your friends to write to us, and get phone co. people to get in touch with us. See 'ya in Miami, phreaks!

Stay tuned for the Rip-Off Institute!

LETTERS

High-
If you come across a pay phone minus the cash box(large gaping hole in front) put hand in hole find small square hole in top rear of large hole. Insert your good finger(you know which one)in the hole and feel for button(feels familiar,right-like Deja Vu). Push it and any bread up in the machine will be liberated thru hole. There's more than one way to fuck the phone co. It's a great way to get some bread. Bye. B.L.,Pearl River,N.Y.

Dear YIPL,
Here is a tip for people who are going across country. Take along phone numbers on both coasts that won't answer. Whenever you stop near a pay phone tell the operator you want to call the further away of the numbers, and put the coins in the phone. After she returns the money, insist that it didn't come back. Give her the address that you're going to, and when you get there you'll have a lot of refunds waiting. I also think its a good idea to dial operator whenever you're near a pay phone and say that you lost a dime and already made the call, so would they send you the dime. Then select a name at random for them to send it to from the phone book.-Bill

BOYCOTT WAR PRODUCTS

The following products represent the consumer lines of companies now making bombs,guns, or automated warfare systems for use in Southeast Asia. These products, curiously enough, are in many cases a rip-off to American consumers as well. Refuse to buy them, and urge your frinds and relatives to do the same. Tell store managers why you're doing it, also.

General Electric appliances,Hot Point Refrigerators,Stouffer foods and Restaurants,Royal Typewriters, Wilson sporting goods,meats and food products, Four Seasons and Niagara carpet,Remington Rand machines and Remington shavers and appliances,Bostitch staplers,Talon zippers,Gorham silverware,Eaton paper and desk accesories,Spiedel jewelry and watchbands, Shaeffer pens,Skip writing fluid, Amana appliances,Caloric appliances, Paul Revere life insurance,Carte Blanche credit cards,Moffats appliances, Avco Embassy Pictures and records,Avis,Sheraton hotels,Wonder products, Hostess products,Morton frozen foods,Westinghouse appliances,Ford cars, Philco appliances,Autolite car parts,GM cars, Frigidaire appliances,AC spark plugs. (Thanks to National action/research on the Military Industrial Complex).

Published for informational purposes only byThe Youth International Party Line.

SUPPORT CAPTAIN CRUNCH!

As some of you might know from a recent Rolling Stone article, the FBI and the phone co. has arrested the supposed Cap'n Crunch of Blue Box fame for allegedly making a few Box calls. We are now setting up the Cap'n Crunch Defense Fund, for the benefit of such obviously political telephone busts. The money will go for support of those harrased and busted for phone co. specials, and for legal and bail fees. Please contribute what you can. It might be you next. If you learn of people needing support of this kind, write to YIPL at once with details. Make checks to Cap'n Crunch Defense Fund,c/o YIPL. This is needed to show our solidarity against facist Ma Bell, so do it today. We will try to have a statement by Cap'n in the next issue.

Published for informational purposes only by Youth Hot Line Reports, Inc.

Address all mail and checks to :

TAP, 152 W. 42 ST, ROOM 418, NY 10036

11

YIPL

THE YOUTH INTERNATIONAL PARTY LINE
NO. 12 AUGUST, 1972

The Phone Phreak Convention on July 29 in New York was interesting indeed. Many newsmen, phreaks, and even a few undercover agents from the Phone Kompany attended, and watched a film about ripping off the phone kompany, ate Bell cookies, discussed in our workshops about circuits, legal questions & general strategies of Ma Bell. We'll be looking forward to the next convention soon. See ya there!

By the way, the film is available for rent, so write to us.

NEW READERS!

If you're a new reader, you might be wondering just what the hell this is all about. YIPL is an anti-profit organization dedicated to people's technology, and we publish inforation that shows you how to fight ack at the computers that run our lives. Every YIPL reader is urged to be a contributing editor, and to send us ideas for stories, information from the inside, and criticism of what we do or don't publish. We're taking a big risk so help us make it worthwhile. Get as many people to join as possible, and help spread the ideas you learn from YIPL.

If you got this as a sample issue, a subscription is $4/year. If you're poor and can't afford it, it's free. So if you can afford it, perhaps you can afford to help pay for some less fortunate person's share. Send stamps or checks but no cash please. We're getting ripped up mail all the time.

There's been a lot of talk about the Red Box, and we promised to reveal just what it is. The Red Box is only an oscillator of 2.2KC, switched on and off electronically, just like a ingle slot pay phone. Circuits will soon be available.
5- 60 ms. pulse.
10-60 ms. on, 60 ms.off, 60 ms. on
25-5 pulses, 35ms. on,35 ms. off

John Thomas Draper, the alleged Captain Crunch of Esquire fame, is about to go on trial in California. The charge is fraud by wire, but the motive behind the indictment is to intimidate every phone phreak in the country and to silence John, who they suspect knows enough to turn Ma Bell into a pile of rubble. John and his lawyer, Jim McMillan are beautiful dudes but they need money to fight this bullshit. If you can, please send some bread to the Captain Crunch Defense Fund, Box 755, Campbell,Ca. 95008, or to the same c/o YIPL,Rm. 504,152 W. 42.St.,NY,NY 10036.

RAMPARTS INFO:

Last month we published a simpler version of the suppressed Ramparts article,"Regulating the Phone Company in your home" and we have heard that a new, experimental system will detect the device being used over 4 minutes in certain locations in New York. This is not confirmed but it really isn't bad news because one can use the device 10 times in a row safely, though we don't think you have to go overboard. Until the rumor is checked out,though, keep all calls under 4 minutes to or from the New York area. All Telco employees should write what they know about this to us soon.

CONSTRUCTION

The Blue box uses two tones per digit. We show one oscillator and a common amplifier, both being turned on when the pushbutton sends +9V thru the diodes, one for each of the two oscillators(for that buttons digit) and one for the amplifier. So diodes are used, or an on-off switch on the amp lets you use only 24 matched silicon. The best speaker is a telephone earpiece. Each tone mixes thru a 12K resistor. 50K sets gain. Entire current drain under 10 milliamps.

Oscillator frequency=1/2x3.14xRxC, when the R/2 pot is adjusted to the point of oscillation. This point has no distortion, and the frequency can be raised, but distortion sets in. For 1500 cycles, and C .0022, R= about 45Kohms. Raising R to 1/X(the next highest standard value) lowers the frequency, and you can now tune up to 1500 Hz. Distortion will be very low. 2C will be .0044, and R/2 will be 22K, so use a 50K pot. With Sprague 192P capacitors, this Twin-T oscillator is really good. Try it!

To simplify the diode jungle, use a matrix by sandwiching the diodes between two pieces of perforated circuit board, one with 13 "buss"lines to the switches and the other with 8 output lines, 7 for oscillators and one for the amplifier. Actually, since 2600 is a single tone, you don't need a diode for it, so matrix can be 12 X 7. The diodes are upright inside the two boards. Watch polarity.

Readers have reported that an integrated circuit exists that used a resistor for each tone, two variable oscillators being required for a box. The Signetics 566 is also reported to be unstable with temperature variations. For plans on building with it, write to Signetics,811 E. Arques Ave., Sunnyvale, Ca. 9-066 and ask for information on the 566 VCO and applications notes. Sign your name Joe Smith,Eng.

TUNING

Notes on an organ will actually work if you use them, but they're best used for tuning. Or,use a touch tone phone for tuning your box, or your signal generator. Play your oscillator and your source of pitch and adjust till "beats" just stop. Remember there are two tones per digit. If you tune with an organ, you must be able to interpolate, that is to set the pitch in between two different organ notes. To set the 900 oscillator, it should be between the A and the A#.

OPERATION

From a pay phone,dial long distance information, or an 800 number, whichever you can get from your city. As call goes thru, press 2600 for one second, and when you hear a click dial desired number, preceeded by KP and followed by ST. Example: KP#156869945ST. Each pulse is the same, as if you were using a pushbutton phone. All pulses must be sent within 10 seconds of disconnect, if not, disconnect and try again. Do not stay on longer than necessary.

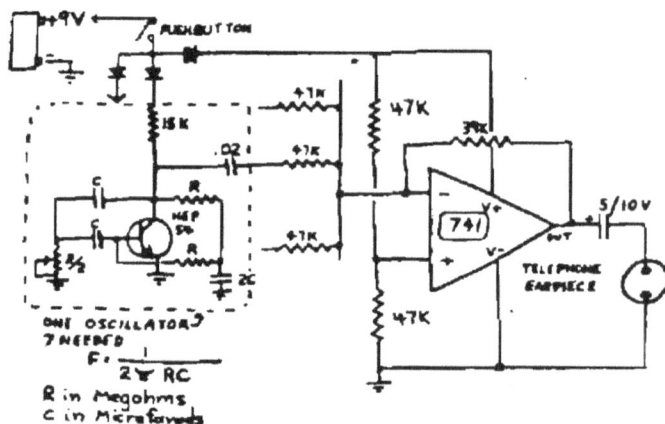

$$F = \frac{1}{2 \pi RC}$$

R in Megohms
C in Microfarads

ONE OSCILLATOR 7 NEEDED

741 OP AMP available at PolyPaks,Box 942E,Lynfield,Mass. 01940 Order 741H, TO-5 case, 2 for 90¢, add 25¢ postage and wait. Write for catalog first as they may require minimum order. All resistors 1/4 watt,5 %. Capacitors recommended-Sprague 192P, silvered mica, or mica(dipped).

The values of R should be between 30K & 150K.

Hep 54, 2N2222, or RCA SK3020 transistors.
Diodes-Matched small signal silicon(1N914)

741 OP AMP - TOP VIEW

14 PIN DIP	TO-5	8 PIN DIP

Blue Box Tones

Digit	Frequencies
1	700+900
2	700+1100
3	900+1100
4	700+1300
5	900+13
6	1100+1.
7	700+1500
8	900+1500
9	1100+1500
0	1300+1500
KP	1100+1700
ST	1500+1700
Disconnect	2600

Organ Notes

Note	Frequency
F#	698
A	880
C#	1109
E	1319
F#	1480
G#	1661
E7	2637

Touch-Tone

	1209	1336	1477
697	1	2	3
770	4	5	6
852	7	8	9
941	*	0	#

A 16 button keyboard with no moving parts, measuring 3X3X 1/2, is available from Environmental Products, Box 406, Lafayette, In. 47902. The price is $7.95 but write for their catalog before you order it. Also, if any readers know where to obtain thinner keyboards, please write us with details. By the way, 16 buttons is perfect for a combination blue box/red box.

Line earpiece with foam, and press it to mouthpiece tightly.
The smartest phone phreaks we know seldom carry their unit with them, but rather a cassette recorder, which they erase after making their call.
All numbers directly dialable are callable with the box. Overseas instructions will be forthcoming.

HOW IT WORKS

There are two basic types of telephone offices thru which all calls are switched. The first is the CO, or Central Office. The wires from your telephone go to your local CO. From there your call is switched to another telephone in the same CO, meaning a local call, or it is switched to a toll office. A toll office, for our purposes, is an "inter-office" office. The toll office connects different CO's to each other.

When you dial a call from your phone, and suppose it happens to be long distance, the digits you dial, whether they are touchtone or dial type pulses, are sent directly to your central office. Most CO's have CAMA, Centralized automatic message accounting. The CAMA machine in the CO records your number, the date and time, and the number you dialed. The record is a punched paper tape. The CO then relays the area code and number to the toll office. The toll office contains a sender, which sends by whatever route is easiest a series of MF, or multifrequency pulses to another toll office in the area you called. These are picked up by an incoming sender, which translates and connects you to the CO dialed. The CO then itself translates the remaining digits and connects you to the line you dialed. When that line answers, a signal is returned all the way down the line to your CO to say that the call is completed. The punched paper tape records this. When you or your friend hang up, a signal is returned to end billing, and this goes on tape too, along with the date and time and both numbers, yours and theirs. At this point the CAMA machine sends the billing details of the call to the real heart of the CAMA, in the Toll office.

Now the way the phone company sends signals on their lines is with frequencies. When an inter-toll line, or trunk, is idle, it has present on it a tone of 2600 cycles. This tone tells senders who are searching for idle trunks that this one is OK to use. When the line is seized and used, the tone is not present.

Control of your telephone line is done by you. When you hang up, the CO relays that to the senders and incoming senders on the trunk and then they disconnect.

If, however, you were to send a 2600 cycle tone down your line, your CO would not do a thing because it isn't designed to react to a 2600 cycle tone. But the intertoll trunks would think you hung up, because 2600 cycles means the line is idle. So they would disconnect you from the CO at the end of the chain. When you release the 2600 tone, the incoming sender would now believe the line has been seized, and will wait for the MF digits.

Meanwhile, back at the CO(yours) the CAMA is billing you for the initial call you made. If it was for information, the rate is zero ¢/minute. However, information calls don't take too long so the people who go over the paper tape at the end of the month may spot something fishy. 800 numbers are a different story, but they'd better be valid. The MF digits and 2600 cycles are passing thru the CO unnoticed all this time.

When you send MF digits, the incoming sender at the far end translates them and routes you to the correct CO, if its in that area code. If it is, and you send the area code along with the other digits, the machine will overload and the call won't go thru. If you had dialed information or a wats line based in a different area from the desired number, the sender will reroute you to that area and then to that number. Most boxers call information in a different city from where they want to call and then send area code with digits to reroute.

Since all calls are shown on the paper tape, a pay phone is the only safe way to go. And be sure to change phones too.

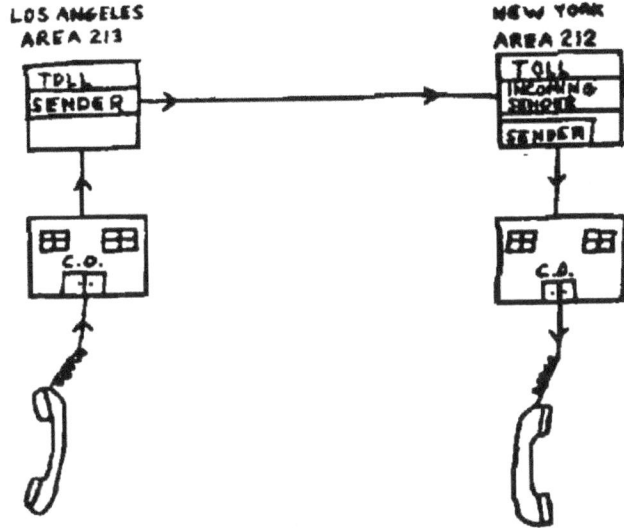

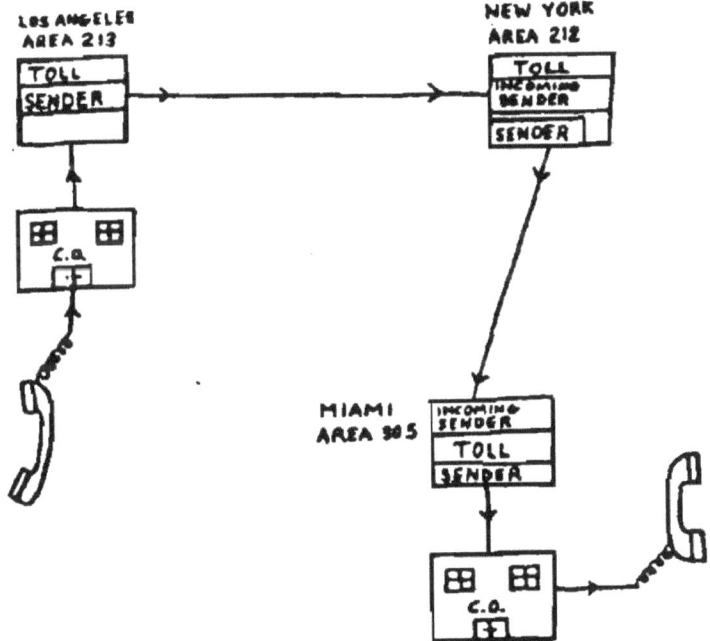

LOS ANGELES
AREA 213

TOLL SENDER

C.O.

NEW YORK
AREA 212

TOLL INCOMING SENDER
SENDER

C.O.

LOS ANGELES
AREA 213

TOLL SENDER

C.O.

NEW YORK
AREA 212

TOLL INCOMING SENDER
SENDER

MIAMI
AREA 305

INCOMING SENDER
TOLL SENDER

C.O.

An item of interest for readers: For $1.50 businesses and schools are equipping themselves with "dial-lock", which fits into the "1" position on a dial phone, which eliminates calls except from dial-lock key holders.(For pushbutton phones, a steel plate covers the buttons-Ed.)

For every piggy action, there is an equal and opposite people reaction. Simply lift the receiver and rapidly push the buttons on the cradle equal to the numbers you would dial. For example, to dial 936-2323 you would push the buttons down(or just one of them) 9 times, 3 times, 6 times, etc.,about as fast as a watch ticks, with a second or so between each digit. Keep count, cause its easy to lose count. Or, push the button 10 times, and you can give the operator the number you want, whether its around the corner or across the country. She is well-trained to assist you most ably. The "dial-lock ads are right, the phone bill is effectively reduced, but it doesn't say whose. L.W., Houston,Texas.

Dear YIPL,
If any YIPL reader has access to info on a pig device called a curdler please publish the description of the resonator tubes. This device is developed in France for use on rioters. Basically it is a tone generator, amplifier, and a hi-fi type exponential horn tweeter fitted with resonator tubes. Supposedly even a hand-held model can cause ear damage and brain hemmoraging through a sort of "sound laser" effect. Come the revolution sympathetic stereos can be turned against the pig. CCS. Yippie!

The Credit Card Computer we reported to you about is not yet available to all operators. So in some areas, the old system of simply matching the 4th digit to the letter still works. We've also heard that on the West Coast,the computor is off from 2-4 a.m. for checking, and credit card calls during that time are assumed to be valid. The same thing is true in other areas, but we don't know the times. They may be the same.

Published for informational purposes only by Youth Hot Line Reports, Inc.

STRENGTH IN NUMBERS!

Sign up all your friends for YIPL. $2 to TAP Room 504, 152 W. 42 St.,NY,NY 10036 When our subscription breaks 1000, we'll have a super article!

BUTTON OFFER

We have these cute little Anti-Bell Buttons to raise some bread, and at 50¢ each they probably will. We'd like to see every person in the country wearing these pretty soon. 10 for $3.

BACK ISSUES
-Credit card calls-How to safely.
-Receive long distance calls free.
-The Blue Box(this issue)
-Pay phone issue
Back issue are back up to 50¢ each, until we raise some more bread.

FROM **TAP**, ROOM 504, 152 W. 42 ST.,N.Y.,N.Y. 10036 (MAIL ONLY)

12

TO:

READERS

Dear Yipl,
Please distribute this little gem of info immed-
iately- "The National Security Agency monitors
and records every trans-Atlantic telephone call."
Source- Ramparts Aug. '72. Also- "Of course,
all trans-Atlantic and trans-Pacific Telephone
calls to or from the U.S. are tapped."

I don't know if the NSA would pass info on to
the FBI about phone phreaks, but its certainly
conceivable that they may.

It seems ITT is pushing Astrofood to school
kids through a subsidiary, Continental Baking.
I think we need to find out just how much ITT
controls. If I get the time I'll go to MLPF&Fs
and check Standard & Poors to see if I can get
the scope of operations of this giant. J.R.,
Atlanta, Ga.

Dear YIPL,
Just a note to give you a few comments on the
August issue(No. 12).

First, the Red Box: you might note that it
is also important to provide a contact and make
the line connections which will ground the tip
side of the line when you beep the box. When a
coin is placed in a pay phone, the mechanism
grounds the tip side for about 1 second; this
is what gets you dial tone on a so-called prepay phone. Then, when dealing with the operator
for longer calls, the beeps tell her that you've
paid, but it will look a little funny if the
equiptment doesn't register the dropping of coins.
Both are necessary for a realistic simulation.

(The terms "tip" and "ring"(also "sleeve")
come from the old manual switchboard days and
describe the connections on a cord plug. These
archaic terms are still used today: the tip
side is the green wire and L1 if things are
hooked up properly; the ring side of the line
is the red wire and L2.)

Second: I have constructed several Blue Boxes
using the Signetics NE 566 IC. I do not recommend it for several reasons: 1. It is designed
to be a voltage-controlled oscillator and is
very good in this role. It is so damned voltage
sensitive that it needs a very stable, rock
solid battery supply. Even with a zener regulator
after the battery, which is getting rather silly,
it is no good because of 2. its temperature sens-
itivity. Using mylar caps and metal-film resistors
I got an 8% variation between 35°F. and 90°F.,
which means you have to re-tune the thing all the
time. Finally, diode variations lead to unreal
differences between tones that should be the
same frequency. Best Wishes, T.V., Calif.

Many telephone services at your fingertips simply
require the correct number to perform for you.
These New York numbers all work in areas of N.Y.,
and many out-of-city and out-of-state readers
will find they work in their neighborhood. We'll
publish Los Angeles and San Francisco numbers
if we receive them soon.
     AREA CODE 212
324-0707 Sweep tone at high level. When comparing
an oscilloscope trace of this tone to another made
at an earlier date, detection of taps is possible.
DE2
HY9 9932 Silent line-Line will be held open while
TW1   off hook without making noise.
XXX-9980 Dial your prefix(first 3 digits) and 9980
and you will get a 6000 cycle tone. It has a slight
tendency toward being permanent, unless the phone
hook is hit twice.
311
958 These numbers,when dialed, read back the number
you are on. Great in apartment basements for finding
your line, or unused free lines waiting to be connected.
660(wait for tone)09(wait)6(hang up)
660-your last 4 digits(wait)1(hang up) RING BACK
6606(wait)6(hang up)
Prefix-9901 Verification. Sound like Telco employee.
or dial 0,ask for "260 official 0-1" and get the
same without even paying a message unit. By the way,
don't use 260, use your own prefix. When verifying
operator comes on say,"Verify such and such please."

New Yorkers are up in arms against the Great
Subway Ripoff. It seems people are buying the
standard electrical knockout boxes at hardware stores, removing the knockouts, and then
filing down the nitch where it was attached. Then
they proceed to use them as tokens in turnstiles.
It turns out that they work in turnstiles almost
anywhere in N.Y. Exceptions are Penn Station. If
the knockout falls through the mechanism, they
follow it with a real token and walk right through.
The 40¢ boxes contain 17 knockouts, each worth
35¢ when filed a bit. YIPL readers are urged to
watch out for these people, as they wipe their
fingerprints off the slugs when they drop them.

Readers who missed the Phirst International
PHONE PHREAK CONVENTION will be able to read
about it in the latest issue of Ramparts
Magazine, and in Telephony, the magazine of
the telephone industry. The Telephony article, though somewhat biased, plugged our
address for company execs, advising them
not to reveal identities when writing us.
Cute, huh? Now we've got AT&Ts execs reading YIPL! However, we applaud Telephony on
the ridiculous accuracy of their name, and
salute their new readers with finger upheld!

MORE BOX PLANS

Correction- The 39K resistor used for setting
the gain of the amplifier in last month's issue is incorrect. It should be between 5 and 6
thousand ohms in value. Too large a value will
cause a buzz in the amplifier from too much gain.

Let's clear up a few details in last month's
Blue Box construction plans. For those of you
without a lot of test equiptment, this might help
you a bit.
1- The Twin T oscillator has maximum stability for
voltage and temperature changes when it is tuned
at least 5% above the initial oscillating frequency
of the oscillator. Otherwise, a voltage drop of a
volt or temperature drop of 20 degrees might turn
it off. For example, tune in your resistor or capacitor values of the 1100 cycle oscillator so that
it starts oscillating at about 1000 or 1050 cycles,
and tune it up to 1100. The starting point of oscillation is always the purest sine wave, but the
oscillator is on the verge of turning off, so a
slight distortion of the wave can and must be tol-
erated in this circuit.
2- Tuning up to a touch tone phone(frequencies given
last month) will result in greater than 1% accuracy.
A hammond organ should be even better. The MF rec-
eivers that process your calls will respond to an
error of 30 cycles or greater with a reorder signal.
That's a wide margin, and it varies from place to
place. So if your tones come closer than 30 cycles
to the correct ones, you will have better success
and less of "I'm sorry, your call did not go thru".
3- Repeat-Call only from pay phones, never from
your home phone! An exception is to call from a
phone that will probably never be boxed on again.
The phone company has records of 800 calls and
555-1212 calls that are abnormally long, and they
have been known to investigate.
4- If your call doesn't go thru, it may be your
tuning, an excess of distortion(tones will sound
very harsh),too loud or soft a tone, extra noise
leaking into the phone, and most important, an
overload in Bell's circuits that night from all
the other blue-boxers making calls. Also remember
that if you initially dial and beep off a 800 or
information number in the area code you will be
boxing, do not key in the area code, just the 7
digits(7D).
5- The diodes are non-critical, small signal units
and don't have to be 1N914. The transistors are
small signal NPN type with HFE of 50 or more. The
transistors mentioned, and many others also will
all work perfectly.

A pure sine wave, from a Twin T oscillator, and
from a touch tone phone, is the best waveshape
for activating Western Electric's brain.

A Twin T oscillator slightly distorted, because
it is tuned 5% higher than its initial frequency
of oscillation. Its stability is excellent. It's
dynamite for boxing.

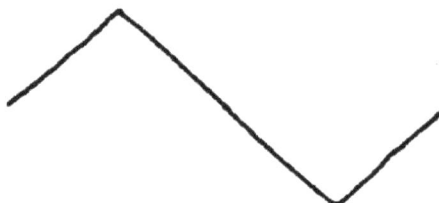

A triangle wave, generated by the Signetics
566 IC(Integrated Circuit). Because it isn't
a pure sine wave, it sounds harsh because it
contains harmonics, and it doesn't work as
well, though it does work.

A square wave, generated by an on-off type
of device such as a multivibrator, has a
lot of harmonics, sounds harsh and is not
as effective as a sine wave, though often
easier to make.

This is a sine wave with its peaks flattened (or cut
off). It causes distortion, harshness, and trouble. A
telephone earpiece has a dual diode connected across the
terminals in newer units, and if the signal level is too
great the diodes absorb the peaks of the sine wave, thus
causing the waveform to distort like this. Remove the
diode before using.

DIALING OVERSEAS CALLS

COUNTRY CODES

ADEN	969	LAOS	856
AFGHANISTAN	93	LEBANON	961
ALBANIA	405	LIBERIA	231
ALGERIA	21	LIBYA	21
AMERICAN SAMOA	684	LUXEMBURG	352
ANGOLA	244	MACAO	853
ARGENTINA	54	MALAGASY	261
AUSTRALIA	61	MALAWI	265
AUSTRIA	43	MALAYSIA	60
BAHRAIN ISLANDS	973	MAURITANIA	222
BASUTOLAND	266	MALI	223
BECHUANALAND	267	MALTA	356
BELGIUM	32	MEXICO	1
BOLIVIA	591	MONGOLIA	854
BRAZIL	55	MOROCCO	212
BRITISH GUIANA	592	MOZAMBIQUE	258
BRITISH SOLOMON IS.	677	NEPAL	977
BULGARIA	403	NETHERLANDS	31
BURMA	95	NEW CALEDONIA	687
BURUNDI	257	NEW HEBRIDES	678
CAMBODIA	855	NEW ZEALAND	64
CANADA	1	NIGER	227
CAPE VERDE IS.	238	NIGERIA	234
CENTRAL AMERICA	1	NORTH RHODESIA	260
CEYLON	94	NORWAY	47
CHANNEL ISLANDS	355	NRUE	688
CHILE	56	PAKISTAN	92
COLUMBIA	57	PARAGUAY	595
COMORES	269	PERU	596
COOK ISLAND	685	PHILIPPINES	63
?A	53	POLAND	48
?RUS	357	PORTUGAL	351
CZECHOSLOVAKIA	42	PORTUGESE GUINEA	245
DAHOMEY	229	PORTUGESE TIMOR	672
DENMARK	45	REUNION	262
ECUADOR	593	ROMANIA	404
EGYPT	20	ST. THOMAS & PRINCE	239
ETHIOPIA	251	SENEGAL	221
FIJI ISLANDS	679	SOUTH RHODESIA	263
FINLAND	401	SOUTH WEST AFRICA	264
FRENCH GUIANA	594	SPAIN	34
FRENCH POLYNESIA	689	SUMALI REP.	252
FRENCH SOMALILAND	253	SURINAM	597
GAMBIA	220	SAUDI ARABIA	966
GHANA	233	SWAZILAND	268
GIBRALTAR	350	SWEDEN	46
GREAT BRITAIN —	44	SWITZERLAND	41
GREECE	30	SYRIA	963
GUAM	682	TAIWAN	86
GUINEA	224	TANZANIA	255
HADRAMANT	975	THAILAND	66
HONG KONG	852	TOGOLESE REP.	228
HUNGARY	402	TONGA	676
ICELAND	354	TUNISIA	21
INDIA	91	TURKEY	36
INDONESIA	62	UGANDA	256
IRAN	98	USA	1
IRAQ	964	USSR	7
IRELAND	353	UPPER VOLTA	226
ISRAEL	972	URUGUAY	598
ITALY	39	VENEZUELA	58
IVORY COAST	225	VIETNAM	84
JAPAN	81	WESTERN SAMOA	683
JORDAN	962	WEST GERMANY	49
KENYA	254	YEMEN	967
?EA	82	YUGOSLAVIA	38
?IT	965		

The procedures for calling overseas are more involved than normal long-distance calls, but they are infinitely far out and become easy with a little practice. We have here a list of all the countries with telephone service and their associated codes. A overseas number consists of country code, city code, and number. The number can be 7 digits, or 6,5, or even 4 digits.

Once you have beeped off your free number, whether information or a Wats line(800), you must route to an international center. Seven of these exist in the U.S.

182 White Plains
183 New York
184 Pittsburgh
185 Jacksonville
186 Oakland
187 Denver
188 Montreal

The international center for Central America is Jacksonville, for South America and part of Europe and Asia is New York, but if you don't know, simply pulse KP 011 XXX ST. You will then receive an international dial tone. The XXX is the derived country code. If the country code has 3 digits, they are the XXX. If the country has a 2 digit code, key in 0XX or 1XX, XX being the country code. The 0 is for satellite, 1 for cable. Sometimes the satellite is busy, and sometimes the country you want is only available by cable. For a single digit country code, key in 0X1 or 1X1. Russia is 071 or 171. The 011 above is an international access code, and will automatically route you to the proper international center.

When you hear international dial tone, key in KP XXX,city code, and number, and ST. Learn to do this in less than 7 seconds. We don't want to waste time on those valuable TASI channels! Often the city code of the largest city is 1, but you can find out by keying KPXXX 121 ST and asking the inward operator for the city code, or KP XXX 131 ST or KP XXX 141 ST for the information operator for the same info. Say,"Overseas city code for Hamburg, please.", or wherever you want.

An international dial tone is a good test for your box's volume. The KP signal should be just loud enough to wipe it out.

If after receiving international dial tone, you key numbers and blow it, you can try again by beeping off, but remember that you must re-key access code to get another international center sender. So each time you beep, key KPO11XXXST, and continue from there. As in regular calls, once you get a connection and hang up on the called party, you must hang up phone, and redial to call again. If you try to beep off a call that has been completed, and redial, you will get a local dial tone within 20 seconds of beeping 2600 cycles.

If talk is cheap, blame it on YIPL!

More information on overseas calling will be upcoming soon as our research and developement team sends it in for publication. Remember, you are the source of our information.

Above is the Bell System's new "musical keyboard." Insert shows the digits of telephone numbers in musical notation, just as they are sent across country.

Playing a tune for a telephone number

Before you talk over some of the new Bell System long distance circuits, your operator presses keys like those shown above, one for each digit in the number of the telephone you are calling. Each key sends out a pair of tones, literally setting the number to music.

In the community you are calling, these tones activate the dial telephone system, to give you the number you want. It is as if the operator reached across the country and dialed the number for you.

This system, one of the newest developments of Bell Telephone Laboratories, is already in use on hundreds of long distance lines radiating from Chicago, Cleveland, New York, Oakland and Philadelphia, and between a number of other communities.

It will be extended steadily in other parts of the country—a growing example of the way Bell Telephone Laboratories are ever finding new ways to give you better, faster telephone service.

BELL TELEPHONE LABORATORIES
Exploring and inventing, devising and perfecting, for continued improvements and economies in telephone service

Published for informational purposes only by Youth Hot Line Reports, Inc.

TIME TO RENEW?

You're never alone with a phone
USE THE PHONE

TO:

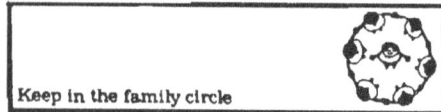

Keep in the family circle
USE THE PHONE

keep in touch with your family and friends—give them a call tonight
USE THE PHONE

november '72 no. 14

HAS ARRIVED

FREE SPEECH

Several readers have advised us that PolyPaks may not be the greatest place for mail ordering. They suggest Solid State Systems, P. O. Box 773, Columbia, Mo. 65201 for 24 hr. shipment or 10% off. Their no. is Toll-Free 800-325-2595.

The following are answers to questions by readers, which for lack of space we must answer this way.

A red box duplicates the coin denomination tones of the new "fortress phones"...If you have problems getting maximum volume from your box (issue 12) try reducing output capacitor to 2 mfd., and raising feedback resistor of op-amp to 10k or greater... Proper volume is when box is just too loud to be comfortably pressed to ear....A five station telephone can handle 5 incoming lines, but does not automatically give you 5 lines if you hook it up to your single number...We've heard you can turn a touch tone phone into a Blue Box, but it appears to be impossible...Thanks case...Blue box detectors are being made, and until we know all they detect, we'll say that use pay phones to be safe.

CREDIT CARDS OF THE MONTH

838-0811-128X, 253-9921-050A,
525-2135-020J, 521-7216-151U
393-3993-088Q, 258-0046-088X
332-8275-126M, 334-5803-126D
633-5411-030D, 633-3607-030Q
466-3325-041Q, 466-3165-041Q
455-2311-128J, 455-2440-128J

The following country codes should be added to the list we published last month.

Afars and Issas	253
Antigua	1
Botswana	267
Bulgaria	359
Cameroon	237
Central African Republic	236
Chad	235
China	86
Congo, Dem. Rep.	243
Congo, Peoples Rep.	242
Costa Rica	506
Dominica	1
El Salvador	503
Equatorial Africa	240
Finland	358
France Fren	33
French Antilles	1
Gabon Republic	241
German Dem. Rep.	37
German, Fed. Rep.	49
Gilbert and Ellice Is.	686
Grenada	1
Guatemala	502
Guyana	592
Holland	31
Honduras	504
Khmer Republic	855
Lesotho	266

Lichtenstein	41-75
Mauritius	230
Mexico	52-1
Mongolia	976
Netherlands Antilles	599
New Guinea and Papua	675
Nicaragua	505
Northern Ireland	44
Panama	507
Qatar	974
Rhodesia	27
Rwanda	250
Scotland	44
Sierra Leone	232
Singapore	65
Solomon Is.	677
Somali Dem. Rep.	252
South Africa	27
Sudan	249
Sultanate of Muscat and Oman	968
Trucial States	971
Turkey	90-36
Vatican	39-6
Wales	44
Wallis and Futuna	681
Yemen, Peoples Dem. Rep.	969
Zambia	260

Also, the following country codes have been changed.

Algeria	213, 214, 215
Libya	218, 219
Tunisia	216, 217

Dear group,
You might be interested to know that in San Francisco you can find out the number of an open line by calling the operator on 222-2222 and telling her you are from frames on an ESS 392 number and what is the number please.

They are requiring all operators who raise from the ranks to another gig to view several interesting films including one where witte itty bitty animated pencils talk to one another about "My operator didn't care for me, she chewed on me and I won't last too long", but the general gist of the films is that you can and will be fired for illegal possesion of CNE Ma Bell Pencil, and that the official communications secrecy act can get you shipped off to Siberia for telling anyone little things about the phone company or it's equiptment.

Real big brother indoctrination techniques.

Another interesting thing out on this coast was that after they spent an ungodly sum to a mathmetician to develope that "new" credit card code the Barb had it printed in about 2 weeks. One phone VP stormed around the SF office swearing and talking about getting even with that "hippie newspaper".

Good luck, and may you have a cheap but good attorney. S. F., San Fran.

CALIFORNIA TEST NUMBERS

A. N. I. (Automatic Number Identification)330 or 6104-1
Loop codes- XXX-0044 and XXX-0045
Silent line- XXX-0047, 8, 9
Loop check generators-XXX-0046
Busy test- XXX-0710
Milliwatt test(tone)-XXX-0020, XX2-0002
Central office-XXX-0015
Suprise!-941-0321 (Los Altos)
Telco employee info-621-4141, 842-9151(L. A.)
Rotary Dial Speed test-Dial ringback(below), hang up and let ring one time, pick up, dial 2, wait for tone, dial 0. Busy=Incorrect speed, Continuous ringing=Dial speed OK.
Ring Back-d105, wait, dial 6 OR
670, 780, 890,or 960 and your last 4 digits(4D)
Step offices-118, wait for tone, hang up.
L. A. Inward Operator-KP 213 121 ST.
Catalina Inward- KP 213 036 121 ST.
Friends at YIPL,
This Black Box detector is probably just bullshit that Bull System is putting out to scare phreaks away. If they have a tap on your line they sure as shit can tell though. I've never heard about any way to detect a black box without direct connection to every phone line, and at $35 per line.... and 7 million phones in N. Y. , that's 245 million bucks. Even capitalists like Ma Bell don't waste a quarter billion to save a couple million.

If phone phreaks want to get in touch with each other, try these Colorado loops. THEY ARE NOT FREE, SO DON'T CALL FROM A HOME PHONE CAUSE THEY' RE LONG DISTANCE.
Area code 303

343-0009 & 343-0068	One of each pair has a
355-8414 & 355-8424	tone, which will stop if
758-0009 & 758-0000	someone then calls the

other number, and then you and they can talk.
We suggest not giving out numbers because they are monitored, but exchange info if you want. And don't stay on long.

YIPL,
I've heard of the curdler(YIPL, no. 12); apparently they're considering dropping the entire matter after it proved powerful enough to "destroy" all the cats and monkeys in an animal room at a large university. S.

Gentlemen:
There once was a guy from Mass
Who trusted not A. P., U. P. I., or Tass.
He took dollars two
And sent them to you
Because he wanted to subscribe to YIPL.
R. R., Mass.

Dear YIPL,
I assume you already know that some telco's are using KP-2 which is 1300+ 1700. Fuck Ma Bell. E. H. , CA.

KP-2 is "transit keypulse" as opposed to KP-1 which is terminal, meaning point of destination. With KP-2 you can call France via England. This is primarily done on overseas calls where direct access is not provided.

In order to stack, or add, your calls up by a long chain, a certain procedure is used which requires the use of blank codes, which allow one to call a number(that is not a customer) in area A and then call again to area B, going through A in the process. If this is of any use(which we doubt) we will publish codes sent us.

Dear YIPL,
Could you tell me where I can get ahold of some information on how to use a blue box on pay phones. Every time I beep off an operator cuts in, so I've been limited to using my friend's phone lines. And because I don't like the idea of making a habit of using a line very often I've just about run out of available lines.

B. P. , Md.

In many areas, operators manually place 800 (Wats) calls, and think you are signalling them when you beep and their switchboard lamp winks. So when that happens try calling long distance information instead. Often the operator(local) stays on a second, so ask for a name, & when you hear local operator leave the line, beep off.

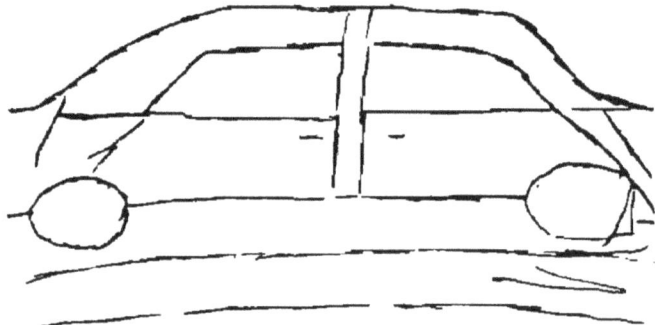

which way is it facing?

THE **AT&T** PAPERS

@ AT&T

American Telephone &
Telegraph Company
195 Broadway, N.Y. 10007
New York, N.Y. 10007
Phone (212) 393-9800

**RESTRICTED
BELL SYSTEM
SECURITY INFORMATION**

subject: Toll Fraud - Y.I.P.L. Publications

date: October 13, 1972

file no [ ] gt.
[ ] other:

to: Security Managers

from: Director-Corporate Security

synopsis: Requests that signed statements be secured from fraud perpetrators who admit that their fraudulent activities were based on information appearing in a Y.I.P.L. newsletter.

* * *

As you are aware, efforts are continuing to effectuate deterrent actions against publications which print detailed instructions regarding methods to commit toll fraud. It has been alleged that information published in the Youth International Party Line (Y.I.P.L.) newspaper was a source document for some acts of fraud.

It would be helpful to acquire evidence to substantiate this allegation. Therefore, it is requested that signed statements (attesting to the source of information) be obtained from fraud perpetrators who admit acting to defraud the telephone companies based on information appearing in Y.I.P.L. newsletters.

A copy of the statement should be forwarded to Mr. G. V. Schacht, A.T.& Security.

J. F. Doherty
Director-Corporate Security

If any of you still have doubts about Ma Bell, J. F. Doherty and his merry band of infected pork, this should clear them up. The above document was recently sneaked out of the AT&T Pentagon especially for YIPL. Examine the second paragraph.

Being the smegma that they are, they cleverly used the word "obtain" for what is really coerce. What they do is to scare people they catch by saying they'll press lighter charges if they fink out on their friends or YIPL. We'd love to tell you they lie, but the fact is that when the Government promises immunity they grant it. So we consulted our lawyers and have discovered something very interesting. The Phone Co. has its own law- Fraud by Wire. You break it, and they don't have to press charges, because it's a federal law. But their scheme backfired this time, because it also means that they cannot make any promises about pressing charges. If they do, and this is what makes this stolen memo important, they are BREAKING THE LAW, OUTRIGHT. And they do it, too, because people don't understand all the facts. They are, exactly:

If you are approached by the phone co., do not tell them a thing, but try to find out what they want, and after they ask you that first question, kick them out. Refuse to say a word. They are not police. They cannot arrest, subpeona, question or even ejaculate. Speak to a lawyer, one who you can relate to. Even if they come with police or campus officials, you do not have to answer any questions or let them in, if they don't have a warrant to search or arrest you, which they usually won't. Too many people have been screwed by trying to outguess or lie to them when they come to talk, so DON'T TALK. TELL THEM YOU WILL NOT SPEAK TO THEM, AND THEY SHOULD GET OUT. This infuriates them more than anything. Make sure your friends read this issue, and understand that when you deal with pigs, you're bound to step in it.

Greetings;
Could you tell me if there is any truth to the rumor
that the phone company is installing voice-tracking
devices to catch people making illegal credit card
calls? R. L., N. Y.

There has been a recent court decision allowing
voiceprint evidence in a gambling case, however not
to our knowledge for credit calls. Often they tape the
call if it sounds suspicious, and play it back to the
parties involved while threatening them. So if you
don't sound like a businessman or woman, or tell
your friend over the phone that it's a phony card,
they might hear. Don't use names or phone #'s, and
you'll never be hassled. Always dial the call from
a pay phone, dial direct with a 0 first, say "Credit
card, 253-9921--050A". You may be asked the # of
the pay phone you're at. Tell her, and change the last
digit or two. She may try that number and come back
on, if so hang up and change phones. Always sound
middle-aged, and in a hurry and pissed at operators,
but willing to give her one chance.

Friends,
Here's a recipe that tastes great and is the cheapest source of protein. Nothing is cheaper than
canned mackeral. It costs 23¢ to 29¢ per pound!
Mackeral doesn't plug your pipes with fatty acids
the way hamburger does.

Add 1/2 can of mackeral to 1/2 cup of Crunchy
Granola to 1/2 can mushroom soup. Stir & heat
till it just starts bubbling.

Or use mackeral as a sandwich spread. For ing-
redients use salad dressing, chopped onion, chopped
celery, a little vinegar, mustard, salt and of course
mackeral. Mix well. Go to your day old bakery and
get rye, pumpernickle, wheat at half price or less.
But avoid Wonder Bread & Hostess: this is an ITT
subsidiary. Day old bread makes great toast. If you
want to freshen it, put in your refrigerator over night.
It will taste fresh & you won't have to toast it.

Service to the People! M. T., Kentucky

Not to mention what they put in Wonder Bread!
ITT's credit card no. is 893-5579-001D so make
sure never to use it. By showing them how bene-
volent we are, they may stop supplying war materials to kill people, they may stop putting chem-
icals that affect your body in Morton frozen foods,
and wouldn't that be great?

SUPPORT THIS BROTHER

Captain Crunch, as John Draper is alleged to be,
goes to trial on November 28. The legal fees
for the trial and any appeals are substantial, and
John is not exactly loaded. This is an important
test case for all of us, because without support, Ma
Bell will win the right to wiretap illegally and get
away with it. Many of you have sent money and we
all, including John, appreciate it but he needs much,
much more. Please send what ever you can to the
Cap'n Crunch Defense Fund, Box 755, Campbell,
Ca. 95008. Maybe you might donate a portion of the
money YIPL helps you save on your phone bills.

1973

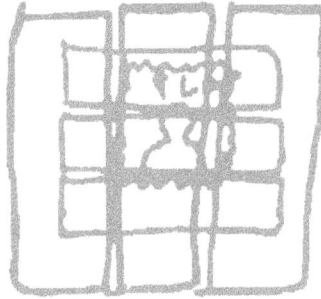

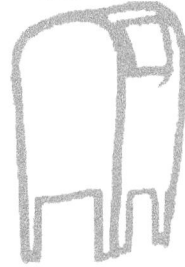

① COVER STAMP WITH TAPE, STICKY PART UP.

② COVER TAPE WITH TAPE, STICKY PART DOWN.

③ MAIL TO YIPL.

↑ THIS IS ONLY MEANT AS AN EXPOSÉ. DO NOT DO THIS, IT IS ILLEGAL, BECAUSE IT IS FREE.

STRAIGHT FROM THE TAP COMES AMERICA'S FAVORITE FAMILY MONTHLY

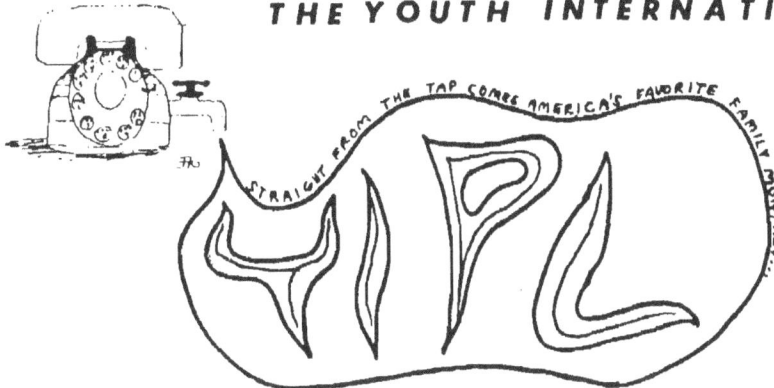

Well, it's a new year, and I feel many of you want to know the full story behind YIPL. My name is Al Bell, and a few of us started this on Mayday, in 1971. YIPL is the result of one phone phreak's realization that the Military-Industrial Komplex is not just a term you learn in school, but a force that controls the planet Earth from the country America. It became apparent to me that the vast majority of people are being used as pawns, as slaves to make a few multi-million-aires even richer. It's all done through MIC, whose main tactic is Divide and Conquer. Most people don't agree with me, thus proving how effective that tactic is. So people war with each other, and the pigs get richer. And one company has accumulated such an impressive shelf of pork that this ⌐mpany, more than any other company, represents the robber-barrons that dare to defecate on our world. This company is, in fact, the largest company in the World. Ma Bell is a mother of a fucker.

Though we are quite effective in helping people to steal back what is rightfully theirs, and we have also truly given a veritable kick in the groin, our purpose is mainly to make people think the question, "Why are they ripping off the phone company?", because once they do the answer will be obvious. YIPL members are actors in a play, and the world is watching. And we're having a lot of fun!

1973 looks like the year of the climax. The phone company's on our ass but if they touch us it won't be quietly. A lot of people hate the phone company from down deep, but they've never really given it enough thought to link it with world problems. If YIPL goes on trial, people are going to ask themselves questions, and that's all we want.

YIPL has in the past been too difficult to understand, and we're trying to understand. Often we've been technically sim-pleminded, and we apologise to the numerous geniuses out there who patiently write in and tell us, but we're learning. Basically we're trying to digest the hard stuff, and print in simpler terms for use by beginners up. But there are lots of things all of us can do. For example, Ma Bells new ways of catching blue boxers will be fouled up if we put in false indications of a BB. One way is to pick up your phone, and all your friends, dial long-distance info, and whistling 2600 cycles for a second and hanging up. This causes many wasted man-hours until they realize it was a false alarm. If we all do this from time to time, the BB detectors will be use-ss. And don't worry, it's legal to whistle. And fun, too!

ɔur friends will dig doing it, and showing other people how also. 2600, by the way, is the highest "E" on a 88 key piano. Practice on an info operator, and when you hear a click after your whistle, you've hit it.

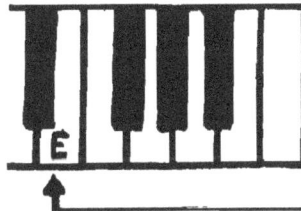

This is a picture of the top notes of a standard piano. The E note is 2637 cycles, slightly higher than the long-distance disconnect frequency.

Just about everyone has something to offer to a reader-supplied newsletter. Ripoffs, recipes, credit card codes, loop numbers, test numbers, outrageous news, computor passwords, overseas city codes, impending investigations, and anything else you'd like to share. We're never amazed too much by you people, you're all fantastic. If you're at all worried about being traced, write us on a business or school typewriter. We'll destroy your letter immediately if you want us to.

YIPL needs more readers. Okay? Please help us, your-selves, and your friends by having all your friends subscribe now, especially if they're in the midwest, Canada, Florida, Northern New England, and Louisiana, Georgia, Carolina, and Kentucky. We need to round out our distribution.

Don't miss the opportunity! There is only one YIPL. Help make it great.

The PHONE COM- The PUBLIC The REGULATORY COM-
PANY has its say... is forced to pay... MISSION mumbles "ofk."

Several readers have written us regarding last month's highway robbery of the American people by AT&T and the Public Screwing Commission. We feel it inappropriate to comment on the rate increase as we are not affected by the new rates. Yippie!

A SURE CURE FOR MESSAGE UNITS

The major cause of high phone bills are those little message units. The only areas with unlimited outgoing service are the golden ghettos; those who could afford it but don't have to pay. Anyway, you can get around many of those annoying message units with the Black Box, also known as a mute, an Agnew, an incoming device. The versatile YIPL model is the simplest unit you can build, if you haven't done so, get issue no. 11 and do it.

The Black Box won't let you receive calls free unless they are long distance. If they're local, and you answer on "Free" you'll be disconnected in up to 20 seconds. However, many times we call friends just for a second to see if they're home, or to tell them to come down an open the door, or pick them up because their train just arrived. These calls often last less than 15 seconds, but they cost message units, and those little buggers add up. (No offense meant). Here's how to do it.

When you're expecting your friend to call, flip switch to "Free" and then pick up. The phone will be ringing loudly in your ear, but you'll be able to hear your friend between the rings. They should loudly give their message, between the rings, and hang up. You can answer them if you want. Even if the phone is tapped, the beauty of this system is that those listening can't tell if the two of you are simply on extensions at the calling party's house! And since your friend hangs up before you answer, of course there is no charge.

Sure, this isn't for long conversations, but it's easy, fun and saves money on those little message units. Even though a special, expensive test unit can detect a black box on your line if they know you already have one, it won't detect it at all if you use it like this for under two minutes, or fifteen rings. Don't hesitate to try it if you have a message unit problem each month. Our black box plans are so easy that anyone, and you too, can build it for one dollar in 30 minutes.

When calling to see if stores are open, friends are home, etc., hang up the second you hear the phone answered and you won't have to pay for the call, EVEN IF THE CALL IS LONG DISTANCE. Works great from pay phones, all of them! Just think, you may never answer your phone again!

READER SUPPLIED INFORMATION

Dear YIPL,
A good source of overseas info is The International Tele-communications Union. Write for their list of Publications. ITU, Place des Nations, 1211-Geneva 20, Switzerland. (15¢) I recommend a)List of operator phrases, b)Instructions for international tele. service, c)List of telephone routes, and d)List of telephone cables.

Dear folks,
If you want a great catalog of telephone equiptment entitled, ironically, "Control by tones" write to Bramco Controls Division, Ledex, Inc., College and South St., Piqua, Ohio, 45356 or phone 513 773-8271. Ask for catalog 303 and Bulletins 201 and 204. Tell them you saw it advertised in Telephony. It contains every possible tone the phone company uses and their EIA code. Keep up the good work. R.A., Tucson, Arizona

Dear Phellow Phreax,
Two queries for you. First: Lets say I wanted to call a transit country. I know I need KP2. How do I go about using it? Second: How do I verify a line once the operator plugs me into a no-test trunk? OH

Oh yes! The "Public" service Commission (should be the Public Screwing Commission) has O.K'd a telco regulation that if you ge two lines in your house, they must be the same type of service. They won't let you get an unlimited and a regular fone. Either one or the other. Must make more bux, you know.

One more thing: If you want to get equiptment, any kind that's used in a home, (touch-tone, trim-line, speaker-phone, card dialer, etc.) get a friend, or yourself, who is moving in a few weeks to have a bunch of goodies installed. If it gets stolen after you move, its not your fault. Ma Bell eats tricky dick, X.

One reader reports that he built a black box and 10,000 ohms was too low to disconnect in his area. If anyone has doubt of their area, test your black box as in the instructions(issue 11). Simply pick up your phone, and when you get a dial tone, switch to "Free". If the dial tone stops, cool, otherwise use a higher resistor, like 12,000 ohms, or 15,000 ohms. Try not to go lower than 10,000 ohms.

For the "Keep up the good work department":
SF Bay Area- Identification number 240, Sometimes plant personnel answer and ask caller to identify self, and then they connect you to computor who reads back your number. Sometimes only during daytime. Ident(Reno)-444, Lake Tahoe-211. SF Bay Area touchtone check is 960-then last 4 digits of your line. When you hear dial tone dial 1 through 0. If tones and levels correct, "beep-beep" will follow. Dial 2 and hang up, and will ring back.

If it is true that Bell is making a record of incoming calls to called numbers ringing for more than 5 minutes, this can be an invitation to really bug them by calling (locally) assorted places-stores at night, outdoor pay phones, etc. Let them ring endlessly and they'll make needless printouts or tie up equiptment doing so. Unable to confirm that they're doing this but at least they're experimenting with it.

Recent trick locally if they have you under suspicion is to have a foreman accompany installer or repairman to your place. Joker is really a security agent and have been known to leave radio bugs on premises, not on phone line. I know of one concealed behind head board in bedroom to get "pillow-talk". Never allow more than one installer on place, or if you have reason not to allow them to enter-someone sick, scarlet fever, etc.

Walnut creek Cal. service desk order recorder 415 937-2762. Codeafone recorder that answers to repairman to call in their time of day ending. These model 700 codeafones will keep recording as long as voice signal incoming. They can be bugged by playing music for max. 45 minutes to fill up tape which they have to wade thru to check for regular info.

Cheap way to get 2 lines in your home at lowest cost in Cal. Get a one party flatrate. Have it put on "vacation rate" which good to max. 7 months that can then be extended indefinitely. Possibility little argument with business office rep that you're on vacation. Use line for outgoing call, at half price. Then order a one party "survival fone" which allows 30 mu. Have the one party flatrate unlisted. The 30 mu. listed and for incoming calls will cost $2.25/mo. The flatrate is $4.80; vacation rate $2.40. Thus you get two lines(one 2-way and one outgoing only) for $4. That's less than the flatrate two-way. Of course the 30 mu. on for outgoing, no extra charge up to 30. Only catch is the "survival" fone not supposed to be in same "living quarters" as other fones, but have it installed in extra bedroom that belongs to a boarder or to your "Aunt Minnie". Have them installed at different times.

Why not call some manufacturers and tell them where to go?
Other anti-phone phreak devices are manufactured by
Hekimian Labs, 322 N. Stonestreet Ave., Rockville, Md.
Tel: 301 424-3160. Also Teltronics, P. O. Box 13, Lakeland
Fla. 33802. Tel:813 683-7409. The Teltronics device only
detects 2600 pulses greater than 0.1 second, but the Hekimian device prints out any number you dial with a Blue Box
after it detects 2600 cycles on the line. Though the device
has only one line capacity, it can be put on the outgoing
lines of a Central Office, and any one of the 10,000 lines
will turn the device on and record the number boxed. Of
course a phoney credit card call will also give them the
number dialed, and we get away with those all the time.
But make sure that if you call friends with a box, they
should not use a box on their line, and don't stay on long
enough to be traced.

DESTRUCTORY ASSISTANCE

YIPL is starting a new service for its readers. If you send us
information, preferably printed matter, or your own plans, etc.,
we will send you back other information. If you want a specific
type of info, let us know and we'll try, but we have almost nothing
right now. Otherwise, we'll send you random information such
as would be printed in YIPL; the same amount that you send us.
However, you must send us a stamped, self-addressed envelope
to hold as much info as you send us. This is going to be a great
way to increase your own library of useful and useless info. Try
it!

BUILD A "T" NETWORK FOR FUN & PROFIT

If you live or work near a pay phone, then you might have
an excellent opportunity waiting for you. It's called the
T network, and it gives you back your money after a
phone call. There are many variations, but right now we'll
explain how it works and the simplest way to do it.

The pay phone stores your money, either to return it or
to deposit it, depending upon whether a + or a - pulse of
130 volts is sent to the phone. The pulse is sent down both
the red and green wires and returns to ground through the
yellow or the black wires, sometimes both. These wires
are in a thin cable usually running along the wall near the
phone. In an inconspicuous way, carefully slice along the
wire, exposing the 4 wires. Move the red and green wires
out of the way, and cut the black and yellow wires, then strip
off 3/4" of insulation from all four cut ends. Tie the Y & B
on the phone side together, and do the same for the other pair.
Touch the two twisted pairs together now, and dial direct a
long distance call. When the operator comes on, deposit the

amount she asks for. While talking to your friend, disconnect the two pairs, because after approximately 2 minutes
and 40 seconds, the pulse will come to collect your initial
deposit. However, the pulse will no longer be able to flow
through the phone because you disconnected the ground wires.
It's best to hang up when the operator comes on after 3 minutes and says "End of initial period, signal when through". Now
wait to make sure another pulse doesn't collect your money,
for at least ten seconds. Then pick up the phone again, and
re-connect the wires. You will get a dial tone, so hang up
and JACK POT, all your money will come down again.

Since the phone company usually knows how much there
should be in the phone at collection time, they will notice
something amiss. However, you can pull this off for a few
months and up to a few hundred dollars in calls and then be
sure never to do it again, because if they find your broken
wires, they'll stakeout the phone to catch you. Best to do it
for only 4 weeks and then stop for 6 months.

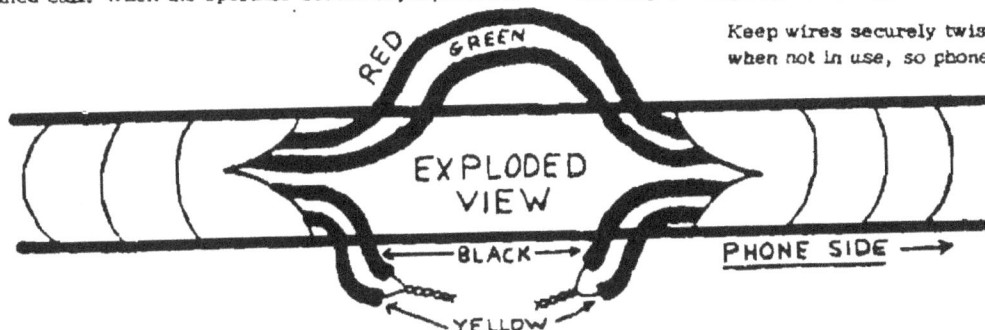

Keep wires securely twisted together
when not in use, so phone works o. k.

RED GREEN
EXPLODED VIEW
BLACK — PHONE SIDE →
YELLOW

John Draper, alleged to be Captain Crunch, pleaded no contest
to Toll Fraud charges on November 28 and received a $1000 fine
and 5 years probation. John's glad the whole thing is over, even
though the plea bargaining was a little unfairly balanced. Anyway
the real Captain Crunch informs us that the busy test for San
Jose is 1999, and that if any of our readers getting an overseas
trunk by dialing KP 011 XXX ST they should realize that 011 will
only work on IOTC accessable lines, such as N.Y. or California
information. Most 800 numbers will not accept 011. The Captain
also says that stacking trunks is now too dangerous and has no
useful purposes.

1973 CREDIT CODE

New! The New Credit Card Code is the same as last year's
except the code letters are different and the letter stands
for the 7th digit(last) of the telephone number.
Example-941-5430-126N-Honeywell of Minneapolis.

U	R	W	E	L	K	H	A	Z	N
1	2	3	4	5	6	7	8	9	0

Follow the number of a pig corporation with the code
number for the city it's in. Add the letter for the last
digit of the phone number and read our Credit Card
fact sheet.
That's all there is to it!
N.Y.-072,074,021 L.A.-182 Detroit-096,083
Atlanta-035 Boston-001 Houston-151 Miami-044

British Phone System Rigged For Free Calls

LONDON (AP) — Police are on the trail of the phantom who
rigged a British city's telephone exchange so that 1,000 students
could make calls all over the world for free.

Government investigators traced the secret wiring in the
ancient southwest England city of Bath last month.

But they fear the phantom has already wired up other cities
for free calls that are costing the Post Office, which operates
Britain's telephone system, a fortune in lost revenue.

And worse, they believe there may be more than one phantom.

"This is a serious national problem," a Post Office spokesman said. "We are making investigations in other towns all
over the country to get to the bottom of this fraud."

The Bath affair was the first "dial a diddle" fraud investigators had cracked.

They found that the Kingshead exchange in the historic city,
which dates back to Roman Times, had been illegally wired and
that at least 1,000 students at the university there knew about it.

Investigators installed a monitor that enabled them to trace
the illegal calls and trap nine students. Each was fined a nomi-
nal two pounds, or $4.76, last week for "dishonestly obtaining
electricity from the Post Office."

But the university's students and many townspeople knew
the special dialing code that activated the hook-up to obtain an
open line to anywhere in the world without the call being regis-
tered. Police said the secret circuit was "extensively used."

The president of the university's Student Union Bill Moger,
said: "Just about everyone here knew the code.

"It's been going on for a long time and it seems the Post
Office left it operating to try to catch the people responsible for
putting it there. But they got the wrong people."

Police said there was "insufficient evidence at this stage to
establish the identity of the person or persons responsible."

FREE MONEY

If your address has a number less than 6 next to it, you should
renew your subscription with $2. If you don't, someone(like the
editor) will end up paying for it. If you don't have bread, write us
and we'll renew you anyway.

15

feb. 1973   no.16

ALL NEW

RED BOX

YIPL
you build yourself!

—a complete
at-home learning program
in home entertainment
electronics!

EDITOR ↑

THE YOUTH INTERNATIONAL PARTY LINE

Dear YIPL,

In issue no. 15 the "T" network does not work for the Southern New England Bell Co. system because coin return etc. still works with only <u>red</u> and <u>green</u> wires, even when <u>yellow</u> is cut. (there is no <u>black</u> for S. N. E. T.)

Collect calls are accepted always at a certain pay phone in a dorm. Could this mean that it is being tapped? If so, how can I tell? Is there any way that I still can work the "T" network? -DESTROY- CONNECTICUT.

In certain places the pay phone uses a ground wire seperate from the phone line cable. Look for a wire to a nearby pipe, or to an electric fixture plate. Otherwise, try reversing the polarity of the red and green wires, this should reverse all collect and return signals.

Pay phones that don't start with 99 or 98 in the last four digits are good targets for collect calls. Operators usually don't accept calls to most pay phones because they recognize the #.

Sirs,

In writing to recieve your publications my sole interest was in gaining knowledge about electrical systems. Yet, upon recieving some back issues (ordered 11/72) I have found the political motivation of your organization totally contrary to my own. My interests certainly do not lie in "ripping off" the Bell system. Eventual reform in society must come from more concrete and benefical works (this being the primary idea behind my involvement with UNICEF).

Because of the misunderstanding initiating our contact, I must <u>demand</u> that <u>all</u> further communications cease immediately. -D. C. -N. Y.

YIPL has determined, after exhaustive testing, that the economy has taken a turn toward heaven, thus tempting us to raise our prices. Of course, we wouldn't think of doing that to you, our money-drained devotees. So we decided that the only way to keep YIPL's price down is to increase circulation <u>immediately</u>. That means either every YIPL has to sign up one friend, or a few YIPLs have to sign up several friends. You people are taking part in the greatest man vs. machine drama ever to unfold in the history of civilization, and you can help to make it a lot of fun, so help out, O. K.? Don't forget that the more people we have, the more we have to intimidate Bell with, the more information we get to use and people to use it, and the more people who will save money on expensive calls talking to loved ones(Aw, shucks!).

hot to print!?

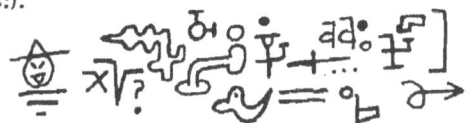

We've only gotten a few responses to our Destructory Assistance department that we introduced last month, which is a shame because we've already got a wealth of great information ready to trade for other phone info. Also we have a special interest in city codes for foreign countries which we're compiling into a master list, along with good telephone numbers to call overseas, which we will be publishing regularly. We've got schematics for various versions of blue and red boxes, and general info on same. So send us info, a stamped self-addressed envelope, and if you want some specific info we'll try to get it for you, as much as you send us. Write "Destructory Assistance" at the head of the letter so we know what its for. Do it today!

THE RED BOX

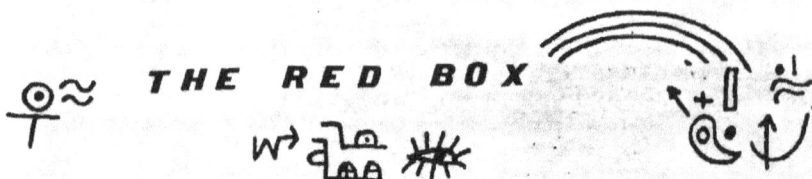

CONSTRUCTION

The largest units in the red box are the telephone earpiece and battery. Since the unit works on 9V and has no coils, 10V parts can be used. The push buttons are high quality units that won't bounce on you and fire the box twice. Grayhill makes some good ones. Snap action are the best, but they make noise when you hold the box up to the phone.

Different earpieces or speakers will produce different volumes. If a low impedance (8-32ohms) speaker is used, less volume and more battery drain will result. Increase the value of the 10 mfd. output capacitor with low impedance speakers, and increase 22K gain resistor if necessary.

Remember, with a red box you are going to play it for an operator who will easily recognise a faulty tone pulse. So make your solder connections tight & use good switches. Cover the speaker holes with a small patch of thin foam to prevent gook from flying into the magnet.

OPERATING PRINCIPLES

The red box consists of four sections, the oscillator, the flip-flop, the timer and the amplifier. To understand how these produce the necessary tones we'll take for example a dime sound. A dime is two pulses of 2200 cycles, each being 60 milleseconds long, with a 60 ms. space between them. When you press the 10¢ button, the flip-flop starts turning on and off, on for 60 ms. and off for 60 ms., continuously. This in turn shorts out the oscillator, producing on and off pulses to be fed to the amplifier and speaker. How do we get only 2 beeps? Well, when you press the button, the timer starts. After 180 ms. it turns off the flip-flop, thus stopping the tones. Other sounds are produced by changing the speed of the flip-flop and the delay of the timer. Also, the two RC pairs of 1M and .047 pulse the timer and the shorting transistor, to start the timer and flip-flop at the same time . Current drain is approx. 7 ma, so don't worry about the battery. You will hear some leakage after the tone sounds if you keep holding the button down, but this is alright if it's faint or if you let go.

TUNING

First, adjust the 30K oscillator trimmer to produce a beep when a button is pushed. Then, simply call a friend at a pay phone and have him deposit money. Tune the oscillator to the same pitch as the beeps you hear. If the oscillator is too high, raise the .0033 cap to .0047. If the range of the trimmer is too small, add a 30K series resistor.

Now, you should get one, two, and 5 beeps for 5, 10, and 25. If not, you'll need to adjust a bit. If you get only 4 beeps for 25, raise the 620K resistor. This may, however, change the 5 and 10 beeps. The 680K resistor is the number of beeps for the dime, and the 120K is for the 5 button.

The 150K resistor controls the speed of the flip-flop for 25. If you get 5 beeps, but they're too slow compared to the phone your friend is at, you can speed them up by lowering it. This will give you more beeps, however, in the same period of time that used to give you 5 beeps. So then you should lower the 620K until you get 5 beeps again, and then check for proper beeps on the other buttons. Always adjust 25 first, then do 5 and 10.

5¢ = 60 on
10¢= 60 on, 60 off, 60 on
25¢= 35 on, 35 off(5 times)

CALLING

Go to a pay phone, dial your number direct(after depositing a dime)(or 20¢) and when the operator comes on she'll ask for more money, and possibly even return your dime. Now, very slowly and quietly put the red box up to the mouthpiece and press one button per coin, and be sure to pause several seconds in between each coin, just as if you were reaching for the money in your pocket and fumbling to put in the coins. If the operator gets suspicious it could be for two reasons; first, you may be off tune or off speed. In that case tune it. Second, the operator may be suspicious because in some areas a visual indication of insertion of coins is provided for the operator.. So the operator may say something like "I'm sorry, sir, but that didn't register". Just mosey along to another phone booth. You'll find the red box is the safest box to use and easy and fun to use, too. Even the operator will thank you!

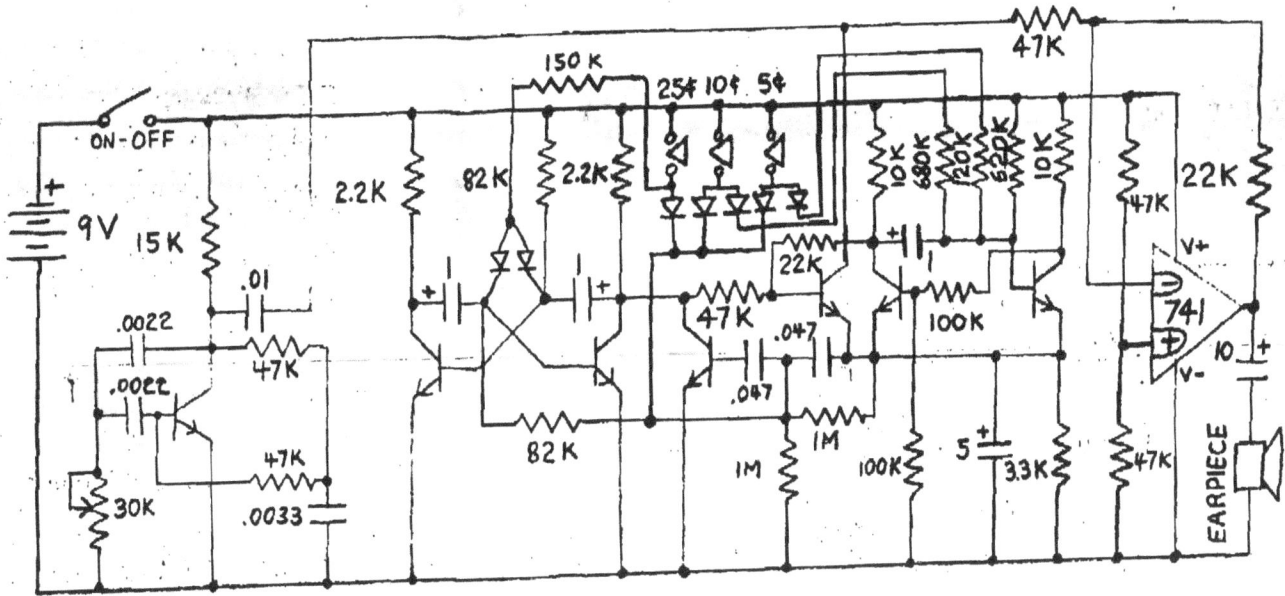

All resistors are in ohms, 1/4 Watt, 5%. Capacitors above or equal to 1 Mfd. are electrolytic. Smaller capacitors should be epoxy or mylar hi-quality capacitors.

Earpiece is a standard phone earpiece, and diodes are small signal, silicon, similar to 1N914 or anything else.

Transistors are all 2N2222, or SK3020, or Hep 55.

· · NEWS PHONE

TEL-COM is a computer designed by two San Francisco engineers. It is essentially a telephone caller with a recorded message. It can be programmed to call up to 50,000 homes before being reprogrammed. Oh yes, if your line is busy it waits and calls you back. A lot of laughs when your taking a bath, or just sleeping around the house. (sic!)... Then there's the "fone freak foiler foiler" which is merely asking phone-phreaks everywhere to spend a few minutes everyday dialing long distance info and whistling (or blue boxing) 2600 Hz and after getting an open line hanging up. This will activate the telephone company's foiler with a false alarm. If enough people do this, well you know the answer to this one... A recent Bell Telephone campaign and PR sheet claimed that 90% of all coin phones, in New York, were in working order at any given time. However, a recent YIPL survey of coin phones in the Manhattan area showed 83% out of order... The name of a Midtown restaurant, Ma Bells. We decided to go in and try the specialty of the house, fried onion rings. Although there were many empty tables they told us we would have to wait because they were too busy. We finally got a seat but had to explain so many times to the waitress what we wanted that we blew another 15 minutes. Finally the waitress came back with the wrong order. The bill for just one order of onion rings was unbelieveably high, due they said to hidden costs. (it was nice of them to let us know they couldn't tell us what the hidden costs were) Since we never got the onion rings we refused to pay. A big burly looking bouncer stepped up next to us and told us we'd have to pay, but that next time we came here and ordered onion rings we'd have credit. They couldn't understand that next time we'd make our own onion rings.

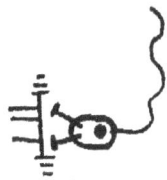

IMPORTANT NOTICE

...about the enclosed 1973 telephone credit card.

To make certain no unauthorized person is using your card, the telephone operators who handle credit card calls may ask you a question or two whenever you place such a call.

They're the type of question that can be answered easily and quickly by a person having a credit card, but should discourage an unauthorized user from trying to complete the call.

We hope you'll understand that our operators will be doing this for your protection and ours.

As an added precaution we urge you to treat this card as you do your other credit cards:

● Notify your Business Office representative at once if it is lost or stolen.

● Do not give the card or number to anyone else to use.

Thank you for your cooperation.

(A) New York Telephone

Since credit card owners are receiving these notices with their new credit cards we can expect to play some games with the operators this year. Don't sweat, the questions are only designed to scare you and make you hang up, thus giving it away. Though you might get a few questions like the name of the company, city or area code of the credit card number, you'll have no problem if you keep cool. The operator knows at most the name of the city and area code, not the company's name. So have your number memorized, and if you need the code numbers for certain cities, get YIPL #8, and be sure to read our reprint on making credit card calls. Also write in and tell us what kind of questions operators are asking in your part of the country.

Dear Friends,

Just finished reading "Happiness is a Blue Box" in the Yipster Times and all I can say is here is my 2 dollars for the YIPL.

Off the subject of phones, tape recorders can be a powerful tool in challenging your construct of the world and to understand how words manipulate (which can be used to your advantage). Tape recorders can be used for social change. For fairly extensive experiments with the tape recorder, read "THE JOB" by William Burroughs (Naked Lunch) published by Grove Press. Only in hardcover to the best of my knowledge, but some libraries have it. Read "THE JOB" if at all possible-most exciting book I have come across in many a year.
-YOURS TRULY C. K. -MICHIGAN.

Dear YIPL

You might tell your readers that it's illegal to: cheat some of the old tray-type change machines by slitting a dollar bill [¢] so the little lever goes thru instead of pushing it into the hopper; bend the tail off one type of pop-top and use it for a nickel in a parking meter; use any of the standard size pennies turned out by the British mint for sometime colonies (New Zealand, Fiji, Bahamas, West Indies, etc.) as dimes in one-slot phones and other places. You might also stock some other goodies along with the reprints, such as an updated version of E. Blotnick's expose of credit card fraud (the non-telephone type) from Scanlan's.

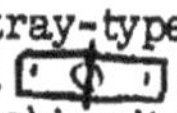

Don Britton's newsletter says DB Ent. was the outfit that offered bluebox plans in POPULAR ELECTRONIC's way back when, and that MF Bell must have gotten addresses of people who ordered them by intercepting first class mail. Bell has been after him ever since, maybe it's why he moved to Hawaii. A local source, who should know, says that mail from overseas is opened (and translated at need) on a regular basis in Oakland. Foreign correspondents should not go unwarned. -FUCK THE PHONE COMPANY R. S. - BERKELEY, CA.

Sirs;

Cancel my sons subscription to your paper immediately, please. He is 14 years of age and has no interest in it. He only subscribed to your paper just to see if it actually existed. Anymore papers mailed to our address will be returned to sender. Thank you. -KH, N. Y. -

Dear YIPL,

For practice dialing overseas: London weather: KP 044 1 246 8091 ST, Australia weather (Sidney): KP 061 3 6064 ST, Australia time: KP 061 2 2074 ST, Free Telephone Co. News Wire Service anywhere in the U. S. and Canada (direct dialed): 212 394-1212. Listen to Helen Banks (sounds like Shirley Booth) and Marian Warshaw give top secret (ha) telephone company news twice a day.
-L. A. -BKLYN, N. Y.

Many times people ask YIPL questions that we don't have the answer to. Questions dealing with what operators know and don't know, how phone traces are done, and general policies of the Bell's crack security gang led by the fearless Joe Doherty and his turtle Flash. We need people to answer questions like whether ESS will allow Blue & Black Boxes in the areas where they live. We need operators to tell us how they know when enough money is put into the phone to fill it up and it has to be dumped. Tell us anything and everything, don't sign your name, and tell us if you don't want us to print the letter. And if you have friends who work for the kompany, have them write us.

YIPL, it is said, has its better days. And although we're doing better in mailing now, the Post Office isn't. YIPL is mailed third class. Now first class goes slow, and even second class doesn't go much faster than osmosis, but we go at the very end of everything else, when we go at all. And there's no sense trying to make it any better because postmen steal your mail, our mail, and everyone else for that matter. So be patient. Allow 2 months for delivery of a newsletter, 1 month for back issues. And do not send cash or stamps through the mail, BECAUSE THE POST OFFICE STEALS IT. OUR MAIL IS CENSORED, RIPPED UP AND STOLEN, AND WE DO NOT RIP ANY OF YOU PEOPLE OFF. But if you send your $2 and we don't get it, we figure you might have forgotten to stick it in the envelope or it might have been stolen. So we ask you to send it in check, or to check if your previous check was cashed. If you don't receive an issue, wait awhile and if the following issue comes, let us know and we'll send you what you missed.

Jean-Luc Godard tells it like it is!

BACK ISSUES-50¢

1- Extensions, conference switches
2- Blue Box Story and Abbie on ripoffs
3- Telecommand Story
4- Pay Phone Issue
5- Blue Box 1 Now obsolete
6- Blue Box 2
7- Tuning your organ
8- Credit card calls and 1972 code
9- Super duper project(See issue 11)
10-
11-Receive long distance calls Free
12-Blue Box Plans
13-International Calls
14-International Calls & AT&T Papers
15-1973 Credit Code, T Network
FACT SHEETS-25¢
How not to get caught making credit calls
Receiving long distance calls Free(Issue 11)
ANTI-BELL BUTTON- 50¢ 10/$3.00
DESTRUCTORY ASSISTANCE- Free-Just send as much info as you want back in a stamped, self-addressed envelope.
Renew if your address has a 7 or less on it.
YIPL, Room 504, 152 W. 42 St., N.Y., N.Y. 10036
Mailing address only, don't send cash, PLEASE!

Dear YIPL,
The ringback numbers for LA vary like mad; however most of LA City uses 6105-6 (a few still use 115-6) but Hollywood (46) has it's own: 810-6.
You can get a high frequency tone by dialing 666-0002. What it's for I don't know.
My question is, how does one reach the verifying operator in LA from 663 (step) or 666 (tone) prefixes? Or better yet, how does one get into the special circuitry (without being detected by Central Control) that Verifying uses? -M. P. - LA, CA.

Allende Accuses ITT in UN

By JERRY CLAPSO
Of The News UN Bureau

Chile's Marxist President Salvador Allende, addressing a packed United Nations General Assembly, accused the International Telephone & Telegraph Co. yesterday of "attempting to bring about a civil war" in his country to retaliate against his nationalization policies.

NEWS photo by Jim Garrett
Chile's President Allende addresses UN General Assembly.

"We are not only enduring a financial blockade, but are also victims of downright aggression," Allende said.

He said United States companies began acting against his government after it nationalized several industries, including copper and telephone communications.

Although he did not attack the U.S. directly, he charged that "capitalistic imperialism" was responsible for his country's ailing and backward economy.

He charged that ITT tried to prevent him from taking office after his 1970 election through a "sinister plan" that included "terrorist attacks planned outside Chile" and which culminated in the assassination of the army commander in chief, Gen. Rene Schneider.

"It was clear that the purpose was to drag us into civil war, the utmost degree of disintegration for our country," Allende said.

1970-71 Documents

Last March, he said, documents had been unearthed in which ITT suggested in 1970 that the U.S. intervene in Chilean affairs. He said another document, dated October 1971, showed that ITT proposed a "new plan of action" aimed at the overthrow of his Socialist government in six months.

Allende said his country was also involved in a struggle against "aggression" by Kennecott Copper Corp.

Kennecott has brought court suits in several Western nations to prevent delivery of Chilean copper. Allende said this caused his country's copper industry grave harm, and its credit rating and drawing power with international, European and U.S. banks have been seriously impaired.

U.S. Ambassador George Bush denied any U.S. involvement in the hassle between Chile, ITT and Kennecott, and told reporters he took exception to Allende's insinuation of indirect U.S. responsibility for alleged economic strangulation of Chile.

AMMO

MARCH-APRIL
1973

no.17

Glancing through the back issues of the NY TIMES from January 1971 to the present has unearthed enough worms in Ma Bell's earth to plant a million seeds of rebellion. Among the strong points in favor of our arguments that Ma Bell has been a major force in moving this country towards inflation is the fact that AT&T decieded to raise the rates for TV program transmission. The rate increase affected all the TV networks. The rise in rates was passed on by the network corporations to the station's commerical sponsors. In many cases the sponsors passed the rate increase on to the consumers. Not only did commerical time cost more, but there was also a noticable increase in the amount of commericals on the network programs. FTC commissioner Jones replied, "TV commericals tend to suggest that use of the advertised product will solve listeners problems and fulfill their ambitions. I see no need to regulate."...Question of the month, has AT&T collected that 1.15 million dollar phone bill owed by the Democratic party since the 1968 convention?... The following are phone facts as reported to the NY TIMES ... Directory assistance service in 1970 reached 497 million, estimates for 1980 are placed at 840 million... Did you know that Ma Bell will soon be charging by the message unit all calls placed to information? AT&T ɔw says the reason for charging for info calls is to ɟrop the work force by 8% (about 8000 people) to meet the rising costs (sic!)...J. Billingsley, a Bell rep, says the phone company is not hiring to reduce the work force...AT&T spent 7.6 Billion dollars on new facilities in 1972...Last year the NYC PSC ordered NY TEL to pay 1.50 monthly rebate to worst service. The company estimated total rebate paid at 15 million annually... FTC study of America's 20 largest cities finds service in Bklyn ranking LAST!...NY TEL, otherwise known as NY MA BELL, holds 23 million dollars in deposits for its customers, yet only has 20 million in debts. This practice goes on in many places around the country...and there has been a growing number of complaints againist the high deposit rates...A US Senate sub-committee on intergov't relations reported that the Pentagon was willing to provide auditors needed by the FCC to carry out its investigation of AT&T rate structures. It seems that every time there is going to be a rate increase the FCC turns its back and uses the excuse that they do not have sufficient money and manpower to investigate. (It's rapidly becoming a trite cliche)...Now, a few months later we pick up the NY TIMES and read a article dated July 22, which states that the Pentagon's telephone bill went up by 4.7 million dollars a year. The Chesapeake and Potomac Telephone Kompany won the increase Nov. 17 from the Virginia CC, but federal officals obtained a restraining order preventing it from taking effect. The federals argued that the rate increase violated the supremacy clause of the United States Constitution. However, the panel ruled that the supremacy clause was not violated ɔecause there was no evidence that the state of Virginia was attempting to restrict the operations of the Federal gov't. The Pentagon, which is situated in Virginia across the Potomac River from Washington now must pay a long distance rate for all calls going into the capital.

DON'T GET BUSTED!

Phone phreaking, perhaps more than any other pastime, requires a great deal of savoir faire. If you want to be free to phreak, you have to know how to watch your step. There is a definite art to speaking on the telephone. For example: it simply isn't cool to call up a friend and speak openly about illegal activities. The chances of a phreak's call being tapped are significant, and your friend won't appreciate it either. Wait for operators to click off before beeping. Other common sense rules include not giving out the names and numbers of other phreaks or those places where phone phreaks hang out or buy their equipment. Listen always for the operator to click off, and even then never assume the line is completely cool. Also remember short frequent calls are more effective than long calls. The fewer times you continue to use the same phone location the cooler it is also.

Many of the phone phreaks whom we know have been busted have known common sense rules in general, but trusted too many people into their confidence. As a rule never let too many people know you are a phone phreak; informing by others is the most common bust. Sometimes these informants turn out to be "friends". If you suspect someone is going to bust you stop phreaking for a while. This goes for any suspicions you might have. If you feel heat merely stop phreaking or find a totally new location.

If you are approached by Ma Bell just say, "I want to talk to my lawyer first." That's all! You do not have to say anything without a lawyer. Find a lawyer you can relate to; it is not to advisable to rap with an ex-DA.

Remember above all that using your home phone for blue boxes is the easiest way to have Ma Bell come knocking at your door. Play it cool, and don't pay.

The People's Bicentennial Commission is a group working towards a Bicentennial celebration that is not the Corporate sales ripoff or the Pro-Administration indoctrination that the American Legion and the White House are attempting to put over on us. Rather, PBC is pushing for a nationwide education on what the values of the American Revolution and the Constitution really were, and how they've been lost. Write to them at 1346 Connecticut Ave. NW, Wash., d.c. 20036. Tell 'em Tommy Jefferson sent you.

RED BOX PHREAKS!

On the single-slot coin phones I have frequently been able to get a dial tone by putting in a nickel and giving the hookswitch a short tap (this takes practice) . The dial won't work, though, so you will have to tap out till to get the operator.

I have built a red box using an oscillator, a telephone earpiece, and an AE phone dial. The shorting contacts of the dial are used to turn on the oscillator when the dial is off normal, and the break contacts are used to short out the output of the oscillator except during the tone pulses. Nickel, dime, and quarter sounds are made by dialing 1, 2, and 5 respectively. (although #6 seems to sound better as a quarter).

On my phone line whenever you dial a toll call (including 800 and info), the polarity of the line is reversed for about a second. If a diode is wired into the line so that it conducts only when the polarity is normal, the phone will be electrically hung up whenever a long distance call is made & can be used like a "dial-lock" but this device is foolproof (but only for long distance).
　　　　　　-H.G. NY-

ED. NOTE: For those of you who want to make a simple and reliable red box, we show a schematic of an oscillator and amplifier and telephone dial. It is basically the same as last month's red box, except that a telephone dial replaces the flip-flop and timer, thus mechanically producing the tones.

All resistors are half watt 10%. Transistor is 2N2222, SK3020 or Hep 54. 30K trimmer is used to adjust frequencies to match that of a pay phone. Remember, pay phone tones are best heard on another phone that has called the pay phone. When listening to an actual pay phone, keep in mind that a quarter produces faster beeps than a nickel or dime. Adjust the speed of the dial to produce accurate nickels or dimes. Then simply force dial to return faster for the quarter (it takes a little practice). If you don't know how to adjust the speed of the dial here's how it's done: on the back of the dial is a governor which looks like a disc brake. The semi-circular brake shoes slow down the dial when not held in tightly by the spring. Tighten the spring for faster dial return. This is tricky on the enclosed governors, but it can be done.

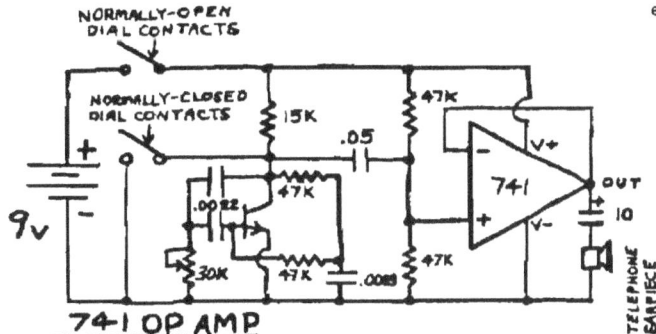

Our Red Box circuit of last month isn't perfect, and we've got a few improvements. First, change the value of the 2.2K flip-flop resistors to 10K ohms. This will cut down your battery drain to less than 4 milliamps.

Secondly, if you're getting strange extra pulses when you continue holding a button down, try putting a 25 mfd. capacitor right across the battery.

Finally, if you experience incomplete turn-on or turn-off of the tones, change the 22K timer output resis' to 47K.

If you want to build a red box but don't know how, YIPL will publish next month instructions for recording the tones perfectly on a cassette tape recorder. Any inexpensive unit will work, but it's easiest to use a cassette with manual recording level controls.

741 OP AMP

JUST THINK WHAT YOU COULD DO IF YOU OWNED WIRES CIRCLING THE ENTIRE PLANET!

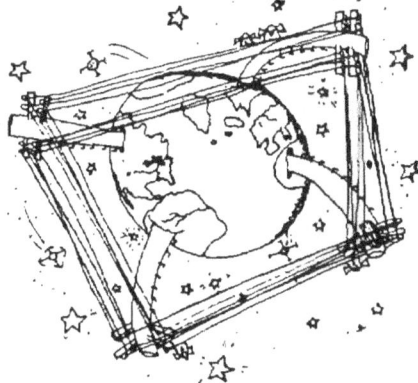

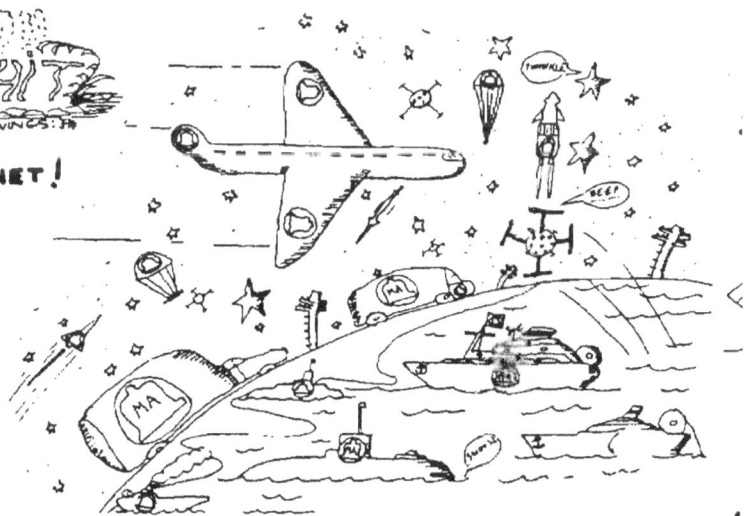

HOLY SHIT

STORY BY AL BELL   DRAWINGS: PH

...AND FLEETS OF VEHICLES EVERYWHERE!

BUILD A LINE RELAY

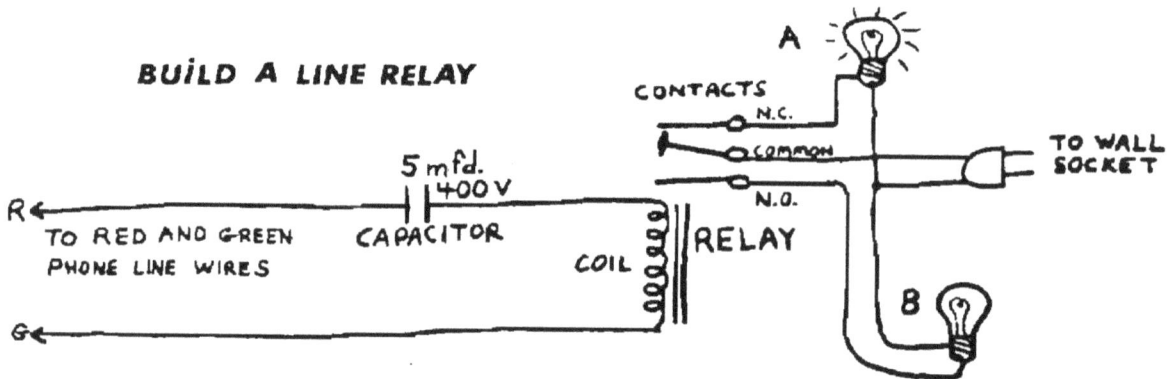

The Line Relay is a simple yet interesting device you can put on your phone line. It will do almost anything you want when your phone rings, such as turn on a light, answer the phone, turn off your stereo, etc. We will show some extension projects in future issues. '

The phone ringing is 90 volts AC , often superimposed on 45 volts DC. This 90 volts will operate a 115 V AC relay, which can in turn supply power from the power lines to any ordinary appliance. The relay is commonly available. However, a capacitor is needed to DC isolate the relay coil from phone line. Without

it the relay will draw a dial tone even with the phone on-hook. The capacitor should be non-electrolytic, and as many microfarads as possible; 5 should do nicely.

The contacts of the relay can operate any circuit you want. The diagram shows how the normally-open and the normally-closed contacts can be used to light Lamp B and extinguish(a good word to know) Lamp A when the phone rings. In order to prevent the relay from "chattering" (vibrating rapidly up & down) you can loosen the relay spring slightly or increase the size of the capacitor.

DEAR YIPL
On the new type pay phones (single slot) you can make a local 10 cent call for a nickel! Just when it's about to hit the triggering mechanism bang on the dial then bang it a few more times than tap the reciever button till you get your dial tone. When you hear the dial tone the dial will not react to it so dial by hitting the reciever button. For example, if the number is 648-6003 tap the button 6 times-4 times-8 times and so on waiting a few seconds between each number. You can also get the number by tapping it 10 times for Operator, in some areas you can get the Operator by tapping out 211.
                    -P. R. BROOKLYN-

JUST THINK WHAT YOU COULD DO IF YOU WERE EVERYWHERE!

CONTINUED NEXT MONTH!

DEAR YIPL
The call back no. in Chicago is 571-6, its the only known no. in existence. Also some new loop nos. work on the supervised-unsupervised method. The last four digits are 9973-74. Any exc. between 271 and 973 are effective. For those that care, here are some switchman nos. (all of this is Chi-town) ED4-9952, LA5-9952. Just screw around with the exchanges and use 9952, and your bound to come up with a switchman somewhere in this city.
Also for those who might like to know, a majority of the system here works on cross 1 paneling. I'm sorry at the passing of the party in N. Y. , back in January. I know, I hung on the night they fucked around with the volume. But no need to worry, I'm in the process of establishing a party line in Chicago!
                    -B from CHICAGO-
Also: the telephone co. news wire service no. printed in issue no. 16 is not free. Here's one in Chicago though that is. (312) 368-8000. Listen in on the Bullshit.

SUGGESTION:
There is one F. F. who has modified a card dialer to send out mf and it sounds fantastic. Can you find out the plans for this modification?
I would like to see a circuit for an automatic sending blue box that can be programmed and then at the press of a button will send mf at exactly the correct speed and for the proper duration with a programmed wait for overseas sender.
                    -ANYWHERE USA-

DEAR YIPL
In the Boulder, Colorado and Denver area dial free 1-200-555-1212 to hear the telephone computer relate your phone number. It could be useful for tapping lines.
                    -AC COLORADO-

Dear YIPL,
I have found out one way to make all the long-distance calls you want from your or your friend's home phone, provided it's not bugged. The desired number is dialed direct. As soon as you hear a click, push down the hang up button several times very quickly for a second or two. An operator should come on the line shortly because apparently by pushing the button you mess up the equipment that is trying to identify your line. Give the operator a number other than your own, but with the same prefix. It is best to use a number that's not in service or of a pay phone so the phone co. won't try to find out who called the number. I tried in Houston, but it didn't work. If it works in your locality-then great! Use it to make long 800 and information calls appear on other people's records, too. Keep up the great work.
-SW TEXAS-

In August of 1970 I called up information and got a man on the line. He said he was information and after a while I got him to tell me how he got on the line.

He told me all you have to do is call 411, wait for the assistant to hang up, and just hold on to the line. Well, I did this and to my surprise people would come on the line asking for information. The line would be completely silent between callers and I wouldn't have to hang up.

There was just a click and I knew someone else was on the line. I did this for 3 days. After that, since 1970 I haven't been able to do it. If anyone knows of this happening, I hope they can tell me how it can be done now.

Also, during the same time period, I used to dial 830-7267 and the line was dead. Once in a while I would hear two people then talk to each other. Any more numbers that do that anymore?
-S. BKLN, N.Y. -

DEAR YIPL
I was reading your article on the T network for pay stations. You can also place free local calls from a prepay station by lifting the receiver and grounding one side of the line. It operates the coin relay allowing you to dial out.

BACK ISSUES-50¢

1- Extensions, conference switches
2- Blue Box Story and Abbie on ripoffs
3- Telecommand Story
4- Pay Phone Issue
5- Blue Box 1
6- Blue Box 2 } Now obsolete(Issue 12)
7- Tuning your organ
8- Credit card calls and 1972 code
9- Super Duper Project (See issue 11)
10-
11-Receiving long distance calls free
12-Blue Box Plans
13-International Calls & Box Plans
14-International Calls & AT&T Papers
15-1973 Credit Code, T Network
16-Red Box Plans
FACT SHEETS-25¢
How not to get caught making credit calls
Receiving long distance calls Free(Issue 11)
ANTI-BELL BUTTON- 50¢ 10/$3.00
DESTRUCTORY ASSISTANCE-Free, just send as much info as you want back in a stamped, self-addressed envelope.
Renew if your address has a 8 or less on it.
YIPL, Room 418, 152 W. 42 St., N.Y., N.Y. 10036
Mailing address only, don't send cash, PLEASE!

17

Dear YIPL-
Here is some info you might be interested in:

L. A. TEST NUMBERS (213)
Reverse Battery Test Prefix-1-Prefix(ex: 555-1-555)
1000 cps Tone Prefix+0002(ex:XXX-0002)
Ascending Tone(No charge) 651-0003, 277-9291, 783-0001
Pacific Telephone Inter-Company Numbers
Switchroom XXX+0000   Tour Office- 621-1779
Frames XXX+0005   Newsline - 621-4141
Hollywood Verifying 467-1111
Beverly Hills, Culver City Verifying 837-1111
Santa Monica 394-1111 (No Charge)
Long Distance Test Board 624-9131
L. A. Trouble Report Center for broken cables 620-5700
Television Control Room(NBC, ABC, CBS) 629-6458
    For people theat call radio stations(for contests and request lines) that have 520 (Prefix) numbers and have problems getting through. Put the "900" area before the number(ex:900-520-XXXX) for people out of L.A. This is a way to call the station for FREE.
POPULAR L. A. TELEPHONE RECORDINGS
ZZZZZZ- 836-5566
RECCO- 836-2125
"IT"- 391-1111
"R"- 454-1904
986-9800- Super Fone
                    -B. LOS ANGELES-

DEAR YIPL
    While living at an Indian Reservation I learned an old Apache phone phreak technique. Simply take a penny and rub it down to the size of a dime. The pavement works well.
                    -JK ARIZONE-

DEAR YIPL,
    Take some plaster of paris and drop a quarter into it. Let it harden, and then very gently take out the quarter. You should have a smooth and accurate mold. Now fill with water and put into the freezer compartment of your refrigerator. When the water freezes you have a piece of ice you can use in all sorts of machines. Sometimes foil or other insulator is used to make it easy to pull out the ice.
                    -BB MISSISSIPPI-

Published for informational purposes only by The Youth International Party Line.

a special   *sex change issue*

no. 18

may 1973

MA BELL
IS REALLY
PA BELL
IN DRAG!

Dear YIPL,
I dig what you're doing and it certainly comes out of having a "high level of consciousness"-so why not be that on all levels? ---and stop using the term "MA BELL". (ok, quit making that face and listen!)
[fir]st, that term is just another way to lay something [neg]ative on females- Mom, Momism, etc. (another dirty name, if you will) and second, we all know its an elite, white, male power group that rules and oppresses all of us ---so c'mon fellows, be really hip and together and change the term (radical women did at least 3 years ago) to "PA BELL"---cause you know there's not one women with any kind of power at AT&T! Keep on keepin on...

     -CC NY-

Dear Brothers and Sisters,
I am writing this letter in an effort to obtain your assistance in putting a *stop* to this neo-Nazi brainwashing S. T. A. R. T. Program here at the U. S. Medical Center, Springfield, Mo. S. T. A. R. T. (Special Treatment and Rehabilitation Training) has been in operation since Sept. 1972. I have been here since Feb., 1973 and I can honestly state that this "program" is only punishment under the guise of treatment; I have personally seen fellow prisoners drugged and brutally beaten for having the courage to stand up as men. If you care to know more about S. T. A. R. T., please let me know. We need your help, in the following manner. 1) Write to Norman A. Carlson, Dir., U. S. Bureau of Prisons; 101 Indiana Ave. N. W., Wash., D. C. 20537 and ask him to either abolish S. T. A. R. T. or make it voluntary. 2) Write to the U. S. Magistrate; U. S. District Court; Western District of Missouri; Springfield, Mo. 65801 and ask him to rule on behalf of the oners who are challenging this "program". We sincerely thank you in advance. Peace and Power,
Note: -Inmate, Missouri-
Call Norman Carlson at (202) 737-8200 ext. 2226 and talk to some surprisingly nice people about your concern.

AMMO

The Carter Phone decision gave birth to the booming "interconnect" industry, allowing manufactures other than Western Electric to produce and sell phone equipment for connection to the phone system, and in place of otherwise high monthly rental rates for BELL equipment. Now, the phone kompany is striking back! They're undercutting their rates for the equivalent independent equipment, and raising the rates upon which they have a monopoly, namely monthly service. This rate - juggling is being rubber stamped by the public service commissions around the kountry. That means that you pay more for your own phon to make up for losses PA BELL sustains strangling free enterprize... Donn Parker, computer scientist at the Stanford Research Institute has investigated one hundred computer-related crimes and "in almost every case there is some new aspect-something that hasn't occurred before. Computer criminals, he said, tend to be "very young, very bright and highly motivated" persons who see no wrong in attacking a large corporation. Their intelligence and motivation, coupled with security techniques far behind the rest of the industry, leave large corporations facing potentially staggering losses of info, computer programs and valuable equipment... The University of Arizona Student Union took AT&T before the FCC, because of their refusal to lease a toll free WATS line to them. WATS is designed, AT&T said for high-volume commerical customers who find it cheaper to buy phone service at a flat rate rather than by the unit call. (English Translation-Quantity discounts for the biggies only, and screw everyone else!)... Ringback for Madison step exchanges 255, 256 is 91911. 251 and 257 are ESS exchanges. Ringback is 978 plus 4 digits plus push switch-hook once and hang up... AT&T has no device to attach to residential phones to prevent unauthorized long distance phone calls. "We frown upon such devices." When asked about the model they offer to large businesses, a Bell service rep said, "Yes we do have that, but cannot install it on private lines." Ever felt like cutting down on the amount of long distance calls made from your phone? One guess why the phone Kompany has no such device for YOU!...A phreak in Wisconsin was recently busted when a central office repairman "overheard" multifrequency tones on the line. Just happened to be passing through... Tel Aviv (AP)-Two international telephone operators in Tel Aviv are looking for new jobs. Premier Golda Meir was on the overseas phone recently, talking with her ambassador to Washington, Yitzhak Rabin. The conversation turned to an article in an American newspaper. "Which newspaper was it in?" Rabin asked. "In the Washington Post," came the unsolicted answer from an operator, one of two who subsequently were fired for eavesdropping.

L. Patrick Gray, Director
YIPL
Dear Pat,
By dialing (212) 797-8079, you can get a recording which will let you practice listening to Australian and Japanese telephone signals.
     -DICK-

NO MORE LONG DISTANCE CALLS!

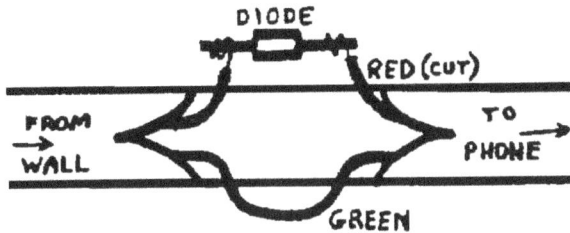

DIODE

RED (CUT)

FROM WALL

TO PHONE

GREEN

Thin touch-tone keyboards with 12 buttons are made by Raytheon 12EF-20457 for $8.25. They can be obtained from Connector Concepts, Box 511, Port Washington, N. Y. 11050. Miniature capacitors, smaller than the Sprague 192P, are made by U. S. Capacitor. Most are available with NPO(zero capacitance change from -55 _ +140 °C.) Address: 2151 N. Lincoln St., Burbank, Ca. 91504.

Many phreaks have expressed the interest in contacting other YIPL readers in their area. However, we won't just give out names to anyone who asks. There may be a way, however, and that is for anyone who wants to meet other phreaks to write us, and we'll pair you up with another phreak who has written us, then we'll write the two of you and let you both know the other persons name and number or adress. If anyone has a better idea, let us know, and we'll announce next month how we're doing it.

This device will prevent outgoing long-distance calls on your telephone or phone line. It was devised by a reader who discovered that the local phone office in his area reverses the polarity of the low-voltage for one second after a long-distance, or operator, or 211 call is dialed. Installing a diode, which does not permit current to flow through it in one direction, prevents this one-second reverse current from flowing and thus the phone acts as if it was hung up for that second. Thus you get a new dial tone. To see if it will work on your line, try it. The diode, which should be at least 100 volts and 1 amp, will give you a dial tone if installed correctly, and will allow no sound at all if you put in backwards. In that case you should reverse the two wires. If you wire a switch across the diode, you can bypass it for special use. A magnetic reed switch in the phone can be used by placing a magnet near the switch for that critical one-second period after dialing the long-distance call. Then the magnet can be removed.

I'm IBM! Try me to Miami!

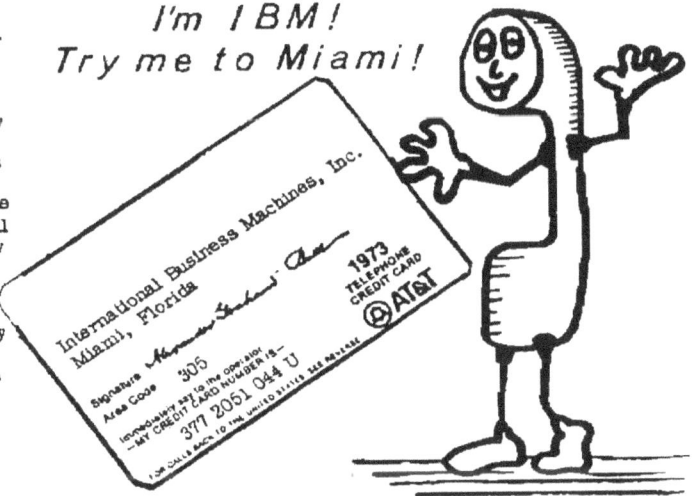

HOLY SHIT
BY AL BELL, JR

WE TRY HARDER

By Abbie Hoffman

Obviously one reason for publishing YIPL has to do with free speech. Free speech like in "why should anyone pay or talking" and Free speech like in "Why shouldn't anyone be allowed to print any kind of information they want including how to rip off the phone company. As revealed in issue no. 14, the phone company is trying to build a case against YIPL. It is also moving on other grounds, namely to convince legislators to pass laws prohibiting the publishing of this info. Many states, notably California have already moved in this area. However, none of these laws has yet to be tested constitutionally. Neither YIPL nor Steal This Book nor any underground publication here has been prevented from publishing any info, namely because there are no New York laws making it illegal. Last year through the determined efforts of Gerald Schutzer ((212)394-4141)extension 3924) Legislative Representative for NYT&T, Assemblyman Robert F. Kelly (D) Brooklyn tried to railroad just such a bill into law. It passed the State Assembly and the Senate with little debate by overwhelming votes, however, Gov. Rockefeller (who uses a blue box) vetoed the bill. His reasons were basically First Amendment. "It does not appear desirable that conversation which might be directed at theft of services be raised to the level of a criminal act per se". Persons in other states fighting similar statutes are advised to get the full text of the ruling. Write to: Executive Chamber, Albany, N.Y. Ask for Memorandum #170 filed with Assembly Bill #10564(6-4-72).

Recently my closest friend had an unusual experience on the phone. He was talking to the receptionist at a major insurance company when a freak connection occured. As 'ear as day they both found themselves listening to a conversation between two big narcotics dealers arranging for an exchange of a brown package containing raw heroin for $300,000 in cash. The person with the heroin was to pull up to a midtown Manhattan newstand in a heavily populated area at 10 minutes before 8:00 P.M. He was to leave the package on the newstand. Simultaneously the other party was to leave the cash in a folded up newspaper on the same newstand. The car was clearly identified as was the place. To make it even heavier, one of the dudes discussed having to bump off two people the night before. It was 4:30 P.M. My friend had 3 hours to come up with a plan. What would you have done? The next 3 hours were jam-packed with excitement and he's currently working on a screenplay about the whole not-to-be-believed event.

What happened will be in the next issue. Maybe.

This is your credit card for 1973.

As we said in the February issue, Pa Bell is making the operators question credit-carders to make the phreaks hang up. So it's good to know the area code and company name, and of course the telephone number which is most always the first 7 digits of the credit card. And don't be surprised to learn that they ask for your name, which can of course be faked. They have the facility for checking out-of-town credit cards only as far as the area code is for the proper RAO code (the last 3 digits), and possibly the company name or number. The only purpose of the interrogation is to discourage, and knowing that the whole thing is easier than ever.

This month we salute the Bureau of Indian Affairs, who confines the original inhabitants of this country to rotten holes called reservations, not allowing the people the right to determine their own futures, while their land is being raped by corporations. The BIA, whose credit card number in Washington, D.C. is 343 1100 032 N (area code 202), and in Los Angeles (area code 213) is 888 2860 184N is partly to blame for the deaths at Wounded Knee, and a continuing policy of Indian genocide.

For credit calls back to the U.S. -Say to the International operator-This is an international credit card call. My credit card number is: 1-F (then repeat your number as usual). From Canada, Bermuda and the Caribbean, 1-F is not required.

DEAR YIPL,
I recently obtained a copy of the party line from a friend, and I am interested in recieving it myself. I think you're doing a great job if you can keep it up. Now for some info, to drive the Nashville info op's out of their gourds try this, dial 615 555 1212 after a few rings a hick operator with a drawl says "What city?" When you say Nashville she connects you with Nashville, thus you are going through one info op to get to another, here's where the fun begins. Ask for WLAC-TV while she is looking that up whistle a short burst of 2600HZ into the phone and the original op starts ringing again while the nashville op is still on the line. This really blows their minds and yours because you are connected with the original op asking "what city?"

You can do this forty or fifty times if your good. Other things to ask for are WSM radio, WLAC-FM, Ramada Inn, Hertz, etc. Here in the majority of the Bay State area the ring back codes are 670, 890, 780, and 960. Identification is 830, also the number to the San Jose communicators are 408 748 7777 and 7487740 also 408. Other communicators are 702 789 6711, 415 630 1212/ 707 482 4000,/ 213 842 9151/ 213 024 7171/ 714 238 3111/ 714 832 8282/ and 714 682 7771 other phun numbers that will get you in touch with most Cal switchboards are local prefix +0010/0015/ 0009/0012/0055, local loops here are prefixed +0044/0045 /0048/0049. For the BB crowd try this routing KP+011+ 044+ST then KP+182+ST, KP +044+834 4799+ST If you can't get an IOTC trunk use this route KP+182+ST/ KP +044+834 4799+ST both routings get you to the same place which is a pay phone in Victoria Station. in London England. Note to all Chief Special Agents: Get Screwed!

The inflationary spiral is taking its toll around the world today, especially in the U.S. We blame greedy corporations, the prime example being AT&T.

With all the profits they are making, why are people borrowing more and saving less? Because, friends, our public utility, the phone company, does not use the profits to improve phone service. As you can see by the chart, more than 45% of your #14 brass washer pays for profit and expenses which are unnecessary in a true public service giving free local service to everyone(marketing, part of accounting, interest, and regressive taxation). In a socialist economy, the phone company wouldn't have to advertise(marketing expenses). It doesn't have to now! There's no competition! As far as taxation goes, a poor person pays the same amount of tax on a monthly basic charge as someone better off, even though the tax goes straight to the government(and to the military waste).

And local telephone service costs the phone company that same 45%! Which means that a socialist economy would provide service improvements like this in the other so-called public utilities in this country.

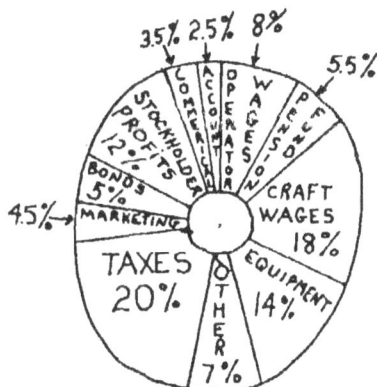

WHERE YOUR
SLUG GOES.

This is the first in a series of monthly articles examining how telephone service may be improved, in both the short and the long range. Write us your ideas.

BACK ISSUES-50¢

1- Extensions, conference switches
2- Blue Box Story and Abbie on ripoffs
3- Telecommand Story
4- Pay Phone Issue
5- Blue Box 1 Now obsolete
6- Blue Box 2
7- Tuning your organ
8- Credit card calls and 1972 code
9- Super duper project(See issue 11)
10-
11-Receive long distance calls Free
12-Blue Box Plans
13-International Calls
14-International Calls & AT&T Papers
15-1973 Credit Code, T Network
16-Red Box Plans
17-Red Box, Line Relay

FACT SHEETS-25¢
How not to get caught making credit calls
Receiving long distance calls Free(Issue 11)
ANTI-BELL BUTTON- 50¢ 10/$3.00
DESTRUCTORY ASSISTANCE- Free-Just
send as much info as you want back in a
stamped, self-addressed envelope.
Renew if your address has a 7 or less on it.
YIPL, Room 504, 152 W. 42 St., N.Y., N.Y. 10036
Mailing address only, don't send cash, PLEASE!

Dear YIPL-
A "Diez Centavos" piece(translation: Ten Centavos) from Mexico, can be used as quarters in ALL pay phones in the U.S. A Ten Centavo piece can be purchased at any bank in Mexico for 3/4 of a cent, or can be purchased in the U.S. at most coin exchanges for about 5¢. (Many banks are coin exchanges-Ed.)
-B. B. CAL.-

YIPL,
Re. #16, p. 3, lower right corner. Telco Info (free)
San Francisco 415-630-1212 San Jose 408-748-7777
Sacramento 916-480-8000 Also Honolulu(not sure if free) 808-533-4426
This is not top secret but designed for Telco employees.
Keep up good work.

YIPL,
On most older exchanges, you can get the phone to ring by dialing 660 then waiting for a whining sound, and only after you hear the whine, dial 6 and hang up. The phone will ring.
If you dial 660, wait for the whine, dial 7 instead of 6, & hang up, the phone will ring in 4 short bursts. Sounds very important, urgent. Keep up the good work.
-M. S. N.Y.-

Dear YIPL,
I called one of the loop nos. in Chicago, and the next afternoon a man from the tel. co. called and asked why I would call a test no., and where I got the no. I said that when I got home there was a written message to call that no., and it was sloppily written and I must have not made it out right. The guy seemed satisfied.
-B. H.-

RENEW

If you subscribed before issue no. 8 and don't renew immediately you won't get the next issue of YIPL. If you cannot afford the two bucks, write us and we'll renew you. And if you from time to time miss an issue, go to your post office and fill out a form. When people start doing something the post office will stop censoring our mail.

Published for informational purposes only by The Youth International Party Line.

YIPL

JUNE 1973   no.19

AMMO

Northwestern Bell Telephone is starting to take the bells out of pay phones to prevent, they claim, collect calls to pay phones and "signal calls" where people hear their phone ring once and call back to a pay phone. Thus, if you have a life-or-death situation where you must be called back, you're out of luck. So much for the argument that "pay phones are a public service"...Robert McCrie, editor of Security Letter, a anti-ripoff newsletter showing companies security methods, is plugging YIPL for business execs. He calls us "a bunch of nuts" and puts in our address with the warning "don't use the office address" (of their company). Security Letter, 475 Fifth Avenue, N.Y., N.Y. 10017. Use an office address-you're writing for a company, remember. Say you want to subscribe to   rity Letter...John D. deButts, chairman of AT&T, in U. S. News and World Report, (Tomorrow's phone service-Why it Will Cost More) comes up with some outrageous statements like "a public telephone is a public service", "Service in New York City today is good" and "we had always felt the Bell System companies were well out ahead in the fairness of our employment practices". Also "People don't visualize the uses for Picturephones". George Orwell did in 1984, but deButts doesn't mention bugging or privacy at all. Another item of interest "Do you have a telephone listed for John D. deButts at 200 E. 66 St?...Yes, that is 421-2277"... "In Kansas City, the existence of just such an arrangement between the telephone company and the chief of police was revealed". That's a quote from Monopoly that YIPL printed in issue #1. Well friends, we all know how big corporations often exert political pressure to help their friends into office, don't we? Nixon just named Clarence M. Kelley, the police chief of Kansas City to be Director of the Federal Bureau of Investigation. Maybe all those wires will go to a little box on Clarence's desk...

MEAT!

Several of you have written about meeting other phreaks in your area. Some feel that this would invite infiltration, and that meeting at electrical supply stores is probably a lot safer. This way you could see who you meet before you meet them. Then again, you don't know if they're in the "field" unless you ask. Others have said that if another phone phreak convention is held, that would be the ideal place. Or, again, YIPL could receive requests to meet oth   phreaks in your area, and send pairs of people the na   nd number of each other simultaneously, from readers whom we feel are cool. If you send in, be patient. We'll try to match another reader, only one, for each request.

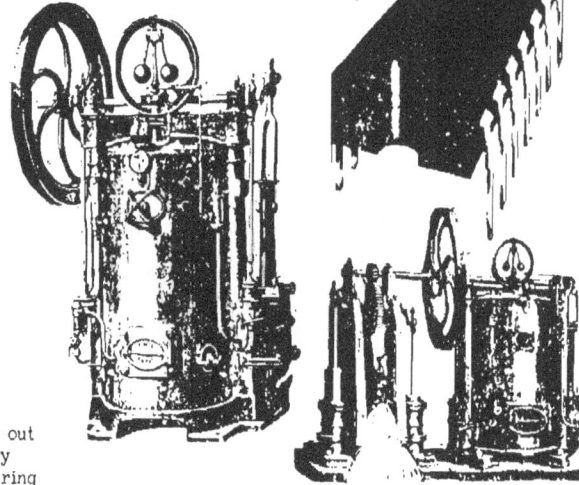

HOT FLASHES-
A friendly Pa Bell worker says that though most telephone kompanies use the amount of resistance in ringing the bells on a line to determine the number of phones connected, in some (college) towns they run spot checks of total line resistances that detect phones even with the bell disconnected. So a good policy is to make up a one-line "conference" call maker (YIPL #1)and to leave the switch in the center-off position when not in use.

MONKEY WARFARE-
The underground warfare against mindless mechanical bandits goes on. After the phone, but high up on the list lies the coin-sucking parking meter. After stalking the little beasties you find they fall into two major types; the egg-headed cranker and the flat-faced change sorter. The flat-faced change sorter was the pioneer of the modern generation of coin suckers. You stuff coins in the side through a single slot; it gages the coin's size and gives you credit for it. The last two coins inserted are visible through two rounded windows(spray paint) and is very gullible. It sucks nickels, dimes, round pop tops, #14 brass washers. Also the larger pop tops with the tails attached and many other bulky items plug it and render it useless till serviced. The egg-headed cranker is more sophisticated. It comes with different slots on the side for different coins, and has a thumb and index crank like a nose on the middle of its face. It is much more selective in what it gives credit for. But #14 washers and, if you use great care, round pop tops if they are both scotch taped can achieve the desired effect. (Be sure to carry something to push them in with like the pop top tab as the tape sometimes stops the "coins" from rolling in far enough.) WARNING: if you use funny money be generous, you don't want a ticket from a meter that is filled with washers. It might lead to embarassing questions).

After tiring of the above methods and wishing to become a mass destroyer of meters, send to Edmund Scientific Co. (300 Edscorp Bldg., Barrington, N. J. 08007) for their mass meter disabler (they call them giant surplus horseshoe magnets). A meter is after all a one-handed clock, and clocks and magnets don't mix. Their monster 5 lb. job concealed in a pack or purse can stop a meter with a couple of rubs. After it is stopped any money deposited will give credit till city demagnetizes it. OFF A METER TODAY, IT'S GOOD FOR YOUR SOUL! AND IT FEELS GOOD TOO.
                    JACK FLASH. IOWA-

A RED BOX IN EVERY POT

If you are one of those readers who would love to build a red box but don't have electronic experience, the tape method is for you. With only a small cassette recorder (price-$25) and a telephone pickup coil(about $2) you can easily and quickly record the sound of pay phone money. The pay phones are now single-slot types which make a tone when you deposit coins, but the earpiece is disconnected momentarily so that you hear nothing. But if you call up a friend and deposit money, he will hear it. He can then record the tones off of his phone, and use them whenever he goes to a pay phone to make long-distance calls.

The usual method is to have your friend call you at the pay phone(one that rings; some don't) and this way you can deposit money and get it back when you hang up, pickup & hang up again. You deposit 6 quarters, 2 dimes, and 2 nickels. The tape can be played to the operator for a sum of $1.80, or rewound quickly for more quarters or dimes or whatever.

Volume is important if the operator is to be fooled. The beeps should be loud and clear, with little background noise. A recorder with Automatic Level (AGC) is good to use for recording. For playback to the operator, a small 2 1/2" external speaker is useful, because you can easily take it away from the mouthpiece of the phone when you want to skip a particular coin sound. The correct volume is set as follows: At the pay phone, alternately play the tape and deposit money, holding the speaker about 1" from the phone mouthpiece. When your friend hears the two at the same level, mark the volume control on the cassette for future use. It's that easy! Use phone booths where people won't see you playing the recorder and become suspicious. And in case your suspicions are aroused, simply erase the tape.

DEAR YIPL

I have some black-box info you might be interested in. This info came from a Bell V. P. talking to his nephew. He says some central Offices have a computer tied in to all its tandems which randomly checks the resistance of the calls going on. When it detects a low-resistance call it prints out all available info, your number, his number, time. Supposedly the second time the same conditions are detected between the same two numbers someone gets screwed, usually be who has the box. I can't say how true all this is, but its plausible, they do have diagnostics equipment. In R. L, (A. C. 401) 959-XXXX (any numbers) gives a high pitch that makes the tandem cheep. 958-XXXX gets some lineman's office. 955-XXXX gives employee new and Bell propoganda.238-0000 gives you a line that doesn't ring or answer. All should be free. It would be a great user service if you could compile and publish a list of what overseas senders go where.

P.S. - I would appreciate it if you could clarify your mail status and how the F. B. I. gets your subscriber's names.

-SAVROK, R. L -

We bulk mail at the post office where they are broken up into different mail bags. From that point the issues are scattered around the country, and our mail gets probably more mishandling than outright censoring, due to sloppily managed postal service. It is also possible that certain individual postmen throw out YIPLs, but if a manager did it as policy it would leak out too fast. Cooperation between the post office and FBI in revealing subscriber names is totally illegal and would be very embarassing if leaked. Not to mention that we will sue all parties involved if it occurs. All you postal workers let us know what treatment YIPL mail gets in your area. We might mention that we do not trade, sell, or otherwise expose our mailing list.

DEAR YIPL

Those individuals who are in the habit of squirting epoxy into pay phone coin slots would be better advised to squirt it into the locks instead. That way the machines will function in case someone needs it. Of course, upright, moral YIPL readers love Pa Bell too much to do such a thing.

-R. F., LA, CAL.-

DEAR YIPL

Only problem with red box #16: faint tone(constant) in background with periodic soft beeps even when no button is depressed. Can anything be done?

I bought what I thought were good quality ($1.30) International rectifier switches (coin silver contacts, etc.) and they're hogwash. Will look for better constructed versions. Thanks for all-you folks are beautiful.

-MM, NY-

You've got a leakage problem. Some possibilities are to decrease the 47K resistor on the base of the shorting transistor, decrease the 22K resistor of the same transistor, or increase the 5 mfd. capacitor in the emitter circuit. Or try this: Move the collector of the shorting transistor to the other side of the .01 mfd. capacitor. This will almost surely load the oscillator beyond hope when the shorting transistor is turned on, but may affect the character of the beeps. It shouldn't be too serious, however.

BUILD A SNOOP LIGHT

CAUTION: THIS IS NOT A FOOLPROOF FONE TAP DETECTOR, but it's great for finding out if all the extensions in your home are hung-up. So if you're going to talk about "Konfidential Matters" or other "Dopee Subjects" you're sure that when you say "I've got it maw" no one else has it too.

To insure that all phones on your end of a conversation are hung-up, construct the very simple line voltage detector shown here. The light bulb is a 5 volt miniature type, such as a 1490 or a no. 27. Ideal is the phone company's own tiny slide-base lamps found in multi-button (hold-button) phones. For these, use a 470 ohm, 1/2 watt resistor to lengthen the life. The capacitor is a 50 mfd., 100 volts or greater electrolytic type. Get the parts out of any radio or electrical store for about $2. Then connect each of the two contacts from the light to the two contact wires of the capacitor, and install both between the blue wire(inside the phone) and the "F" screw, where the blue wire normally connects to. Be careful not to touch other screws or wires with the new parts you install. Carefully wrap up the connections with tape and close up the phone. Test the light by picking up the phone. The light will light, and if someone picks up an extension, it will go very dim or completely out.

HOW IT WORKS: When a fone is in use(without a black box) the voltage on your phone line drops to about 4 volts. If the lamp is wired as shown, the 4 volts will flow through it when the phone is picked up. If another phone is used, the line drops to only 2 volts, and the light gets weaker. This other phone, however, must be on your phone line, and not, for example, on the line of a friend you're talking to. The capacitor allows the high ringing voltage to pass around the lamp, so that the bulb is not accidentally fizzed if the phone is picked up during a ring. You can install this in any normal dial phone, even if already equipped with a black box (Issue 11). The light will not light during free long-distance calls, however since we don't make free long-distance calls that's a minor problem, no?

Well, here we are in the midst of the Watergate, with all kinds of bearings and charges and the like, and everybody trying to see who at the White House is involved, when in fact the real criminals are not even being mentioned! Impossible? Not in korporate Amerika! The AT&T-owned Chesapeake and Potomac Telephone Kompany was in every way part of the Watergate bugging operation. And don't believe for a minute that The Phone Kompany helps police as a rule. AT&T is Nixon's friend, not McGovern's. AT&T makes profits off the war, inflation, and wage controls, just as ITT, related to AT&T only by being a huge ripoff Korporation, and by the fact that ITT's anti-trust bribe makes it the other hidden criminal in Watergate. Nixon and politicians go on trial, but the real criminals go on Welfare-with you footing the bill. ITT's other relationship to AT&T is that they buy used, beat-up phone booths from Bell for South Americans! ITT's Memphis credit card is 525 8406 187 K(Area Code 901) Don't buy Morton frozen shit, Avis, Wonder, Hostess, or stay at a Sheraton Inn. Tell all the people you meet to do the same!

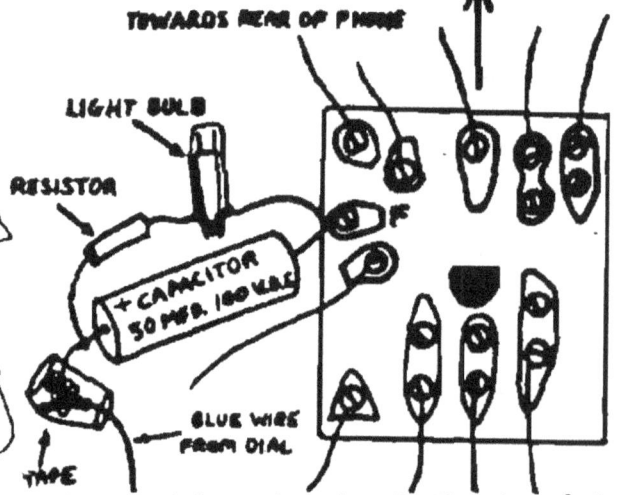

If resistor is not needed, simply replace it with a piece of wire.

YIPL IS

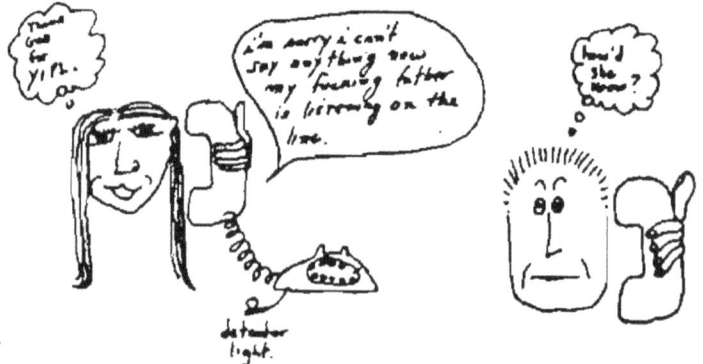

It's not just the rate increases that burn me up about Bell. It's those local calls that sound like there's an atomic war on, after you've dialed a wrong number three times in a row. It's that lousy Bell service.

Lousy service comes from rotten equiptment and asinine employees. The equiptment is rotten because Bell doesn't feel like buying new equiptment. It costs money and doesn't make money for them. Thus, there is no reason. People don't enjoy peircing tones that blow their ears out, or taps and clicks constantly on their private conversations. But people don't count, unless they're the few who own stock, lots of stock. It's a fact that in New York City the phone company puts the new equiptment in the richer areas and badly neglect service in predominantly non-white areas. Recently they sent out printed leaflets in the bills saying that they were changing to a new dial tone to improve service. Result- a new dial tone with no improvement in service.

The employees are another problem. Though there are many polite employees, the bad ones do their best to make up for their numbers. They listen to your conversations, act like they do you a favor, and cut you off if you start to get apoplectic from not being able to strangle them. It has often happened that an operator will accuse you of being a bother or of lying to them, and they then pronounce your sentence- your phone will be disconnected for the night. Too bad you only get credit if service is cut for 24 straight hours. And if you call the business office you get to talk to the latest invention of Bell Laboratories-computor people. They recite certain phrases and no others. Sometimes they blow a fuse and keep repeating phrases in random incoherent tones.

You don't have to be sick to work for Bell; as their ads say, "We'll train you". Why do some operators monitor your calls? Because operators themselves are harassed and monitored by their supervisors, and the supervisors don't make clicks when they listen to you _and_ the operator. Employees are treated like children, like boy scouts, or as if they're in the army (as many employees are hired because they're "pre-disciplined"). Employees are urged to act like they have some personal stake in AT&T and to protect its equiptment with their life. Little insects that eat cloth wire remain a pain in the ass to operators bodies because Pa Bell won't spray their fossilized equiptment or (God forbid!) replace it with plastic wires. Profits before People-AT&T's Success Story!

But cheer up folks! Soon AT&T will eliminate thousands of jobs by charging for information calls, brainwashing us into dialing our own calls, and soon there will just be one big daddy computor*AND THAT'S ALL! Who needs people anyway?

Light and Sound Weapon Tested

LONDON, ENGLAND (AP) — British scientists are testing an anti-riot weapon that uses sound and light waves to induce nausea and epileptic fits to break up mobs, the New Scientist magazine reported Friday.

The magazine said in its description of the weapon: "A large group of protesters reaches police lines. Suddenly 5 per cent of the group has epileptic fits. Although they see and hear nothing strange, the rest feel a throbbing in the ears and a flashing in their eyes and possibly one-quarter become sick. The group panics and disperses."

The New Scientist said the weapon uses invisible infrared light rays combined with ultrasonic sound waves almost inaudible to the human ear. "It has been known for many years that rapidly flashing lights will trigger attacks not only in known epileptics but in about 4 per cent of apparently normal people as well." New Scientist said.

YIPL, c/o TAP, room 418, 152 W. 42 St., NYC
Mailing address only, don't send cash, PLEASE! 10036

HEAD CRASH

Using the same format as "Destructory Assistance", Head Crash will try to distribute info relating to computer systems. WE HAVE- passwords and account numbers, some "operator only" commands for the PDP-10, and a program which will print out all jobs and account numbers under IBM's HASP 360 system.
WE NEED - more account numbers and passwords, listings of cancer, virus, "the green Phantom" etc, and any operator only commands for any system.

R. SYSTAT

BE ALL YOU CAN BE - READ

A case of Steal This Book has been donated to raise money for YIPL and we're offering them at $2.25 each. YIPL also reccommends Monopoly, an amazing look at AT&T that will astound even veteran phreaks with all it's dirt. They're at $1.20 each. Both prices include postage.

YIPL is that kind of thing that you don't subscribe to unless you have to. Since we all have to, it's $4 a year. If you can't afford $4 you really need YIPL so it's free. Renew your subscription if the number next to your address is less than 9. (Free subs must renew also. Just send us a note, please.)

Published for informational purposes only by the Youth International Party Line

YIPL will not demand payment on any item listed if you are short on funds. However this news-fact sheet is supported by your contributions.

19

YOUTH INTERNATIONAL PARTY LINE

JULY 1973

no. 20

YIPL

Dear YIPL:

The New York Telephone Company originally publicized these numbers when it introduced International Direct Distance Dialing (DDD), but for some reason the numbers were not mentioned in the new brochures. Perhaps they felt that these recordings would encourage people to use their boxes for calls to other countries. In any case, here is the complete list of recordings:

FORIEGN TELEPHONE SIGNALS

(212) 363-8888 Norway and Sweden
(212) 363-8889 Italy and Luxembourg
(212) 363-8849 Switzerland and Denmark
(212) 797-8029 Greece and Spain
(212) 797-8079 Australia and Japan
(212) 797-8729 British Isles and France
(212) 797-8798 Belgium and Germany

The local A&P has two pay phones but they ripped out the number plate since the A&P chain doesn't want the public to know the number of the pay phones in their stores. I tried dialing 958 but it didn't work (although it works in [oth]er pay phones). Any ideas why 958 didn't work? Can [A]&P request the telephone company to disconnect the Automatic Number Identification from its phones?

-J. R., N. Y. -

Could be that the exchange of the particular pay phone has another ANI number. Try ringback, the bell may have been deactivated anyway. Complain to the manager that someone might have to reach you while shopping, and you might go to a store that doesn't make already lousy service even worse. But it isn't likely Bell disconnected ANI just from those pay phones.

Also, try reason with the manager, since complaining to the phone company won't do any good. The manager will, however, have a lot of pull with them. Ask the manager how one makes a 10 minute call with one dime. What happens when the dime runs out? Call collect, and pay more? What do they have against calling from home phones back to pay phones? Don't people pay for home service?

Dear YIPL,

Issue #18 gave a Nevada Bell communicator number (702-789-6711) which is NOT a free number, unlike the Pacific Telephone numbers and most of the others. Please notify your readers. The AT&T newsline number(212-732-8030) which is free now will have a new number(will write as soon as I know). Plans are for calls to the new number to be free only from nearby N. Y. and N. J.; if the toll charges from N. J. are 50¢ or less, or the charges from N. Y. are $1.06 or less, the call will be free. Otherwise it will be billed in the usual manner.

-GS, NY-

J. - Since some people are afraid that the FBI or others will find out that they subscribe to YIPL, would it be possible to offer to mail them out in an envelope, first class, for an extra $1 or $2 a year?

Yes- for the extra hassle, though, we'll need $1.50, if you're already paying for a subscription, and as always, free if you're receiving a free subscription.

BE SURE AND BRING AN ISSUE OF YIPL ADDRESSED TO YOU FOR FREE CONVENTION ADMISSION.

A recent rumor flying around Washington was that there was a number, 560-9944, that made a rising siren tone with a click if your phone was tapped, and no click meant no tap. NBC anchorman John Chancellor called the number and heard a click, so he called the phone company. They told him they disconnected it because people were making too many calls to it, falsely thinking that it told of phone taps. An army intelligence source told the N. Y. Post that there was a similar number in N. Y., but he didn't know it. If he had read YIPL #14, however, he would have, 324-0707. This number, to our knowledge, was not a bug detector. It is a test number that swept through the frequencies of the long-distance circuits. When it reaches 2600, there is a momentary click because testmen using it long-distance don't want to be causing extra switching when checking a line. Also, filters in all long-distance trunks would cause the loss of the tone at 2600 anyway. The Telecommand(YIPL #3) detects a tone sent down a line and silently answers the phone. If you suspect a Telecommand on your phone, and were to feed a rising siren tone into your phone, you would hear a click when the frequency of the Telecommand was reached, and the click would mean that the Telecommand had just turned on. Since the chance of a Telecommand being on your phone is small compared to the many more common taps, using the phone company's sweep tone could prove to very misleading, at the very least. Since the rumors began, both the Washington and N. Y. numbers have become busy signals. So it appears that a common test number useful for one limited type of bug detection and no others has bitten the dust.

BACK ISSUES-50¢

1- Extensions, conference switches
2- Blue Box Story and Abbie on ripoffs
3- Telecommand Story
4- Pay Phone Issue
5- Blue Box 1 Now obsolete
6- Blue Box 2
7- Tuning your organ
8- Credit card calls and 1972 code
[9]- Super duper project(See issue 11)
[10]
11- Receive long distance calls Free
12- Blue Box Plans
13- International Calls
14- International Calls & AT&T Papers
15-1973 Credit Code_T Network
16- Red Box Plans
17- Red Box, Line Relay
18- Call Stopper
19- The Snoop Light

FACT SHEETS-25¢
How not to get caught making credit calls
Receiving long distance calls Free(Issue 11)
ANTI-BELL BUTTON- 50¢ 10/$3.00
DESTRUCTORY ASSISTANCE- Free- Just send as much info as you want back in a stamped, self-addressed envelope.
Renew if your address has a 10 or less on it.
YIPL, Room 504, 152 W. 42 St., N. Y., N. Y. 10036
Mailing address only, don't send cash, PLEASE!

IS THE UNITED STATES THE BEST AND HAPPIEST NATION IN THE WORLD?
YES [] NO []

YIPL is free if you can't afford it. If you must renew and can't afford, write us or we have to cancel your subscription.

Head Crash-Send us computor passwords and operator-only codes in return for more of same.

Send a stamped, self-addressed envelope, please.

THE CHEESE BOX

The Cheese Box is simply a conference line, or loop-around. They are very popular with bookies who place bets by phone, because their clients call one number, and the bookie calls another, and police won't find the bookie at the location of either of the two numbers. This is precisely why loops have been a favorite of phone phreaks, too.

Bell's loops are limited because they often disconnect after a certain time, one of the two numbers must be called first, and they are often monitored and sometimes even charged. The Cheese Box can be extended to many lines, thereby creating conferences, and will let either line be called first and hang on indefinitely. Last but certainly not least, the Cheese Box is free.

Phone voltage is normally 45 volts. When the phone rings, a 90 volt AC signal is applied to the line. The zener diode conducts if the voltage rises to 56 volts, thus it conducts as the phone begins to ring, in fact, before the phone rings. As soon as it conducts, the phone equipment thinks you picked up (because current is drawn by the zener) and the voltage drops below the zener voltage, and it stops conducting. All this happens so quickly that essentially the zener conducts for only a few milliseconds, and the billing equipment does not start. If you call from a local pay phone, you will get your dime back. And you can hold on until someone calls in on the other line or lines. When they do, their line will be answered in the same way and you can then talk to each other. The capacitors prevent the DC voltages on the lines from interfering with each other. Either side of the line can affect the line status if allowed to touch another line.

Install the zener diode to the red and green wires of your phone line. If you install it backwards, there will be no dial tone on your phone, if so, reverse the wires from the zener.

A zener diode will conduct electricity when the anode is more positive than the cathode, or when the cathode is more than a certain number of volts more positive than the anode, in this case 56 volts.

Since the phone company has a special hatred for phone attachments that cause free calls, many bookies use the Cheese Box for only a few minutes, since calls over 3 minutes can be detected if the phone company decides to do something about it.

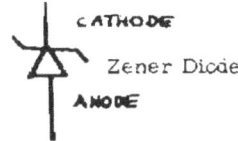

Zener Diode

CATHODE — Zener Diode — ANODE

2-Line Cheese Box

Phone Line A   Phone Line B

.5 Mfd. 100 Volt Capacitors

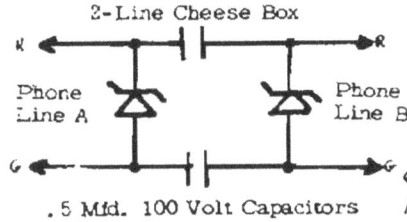

Hotel Diploma
108 W 43 st.
N.Y.C.
Grand Ballroom

3-Line Conferencer

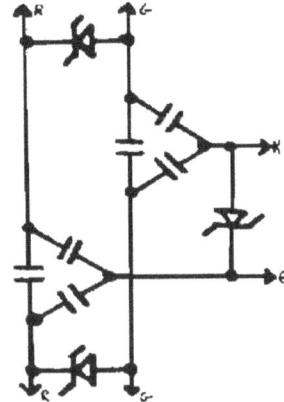

4-Line Conferencer

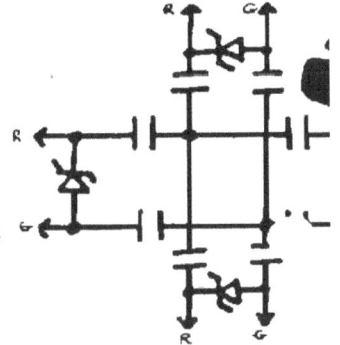

Hi,

Here are some good references on switching systems:
Bell laboratories record Jan. 70   page 13
Bell System Technical Journal Nov. 60 page 1381
This one is the best paper on the Bell switching system and pages 1398, 1400, and 1422 will give you a good understanding of how the toll system works. Page 1422 explains supervision principles. Supervision is returned to the caller when the called party answers. As a result you get billed. If you disconnect (2600) on a toll call after supervision has been returned to you, you will be timed out by your local office. That is, you will lose the circuit in 15-30 seconds. If you are not souped, then disconnecting with 2600 does not cause time out. On what calls are you unsouped? If you call a phone that has a black box or mute, a call to information, service calls, or recorded messages . The phone company does not return supervision on 555-1212 so you will not be charged. Thus only the first billing entry is made. If you MF off of long distance information and call a supervised number, the start and stop of conversation will be recorded That is, you will be billed for a call to information which is IMPOSSIBLE as supervision isn't returned on those calls You went from an unsupervised line to a supervised line during the same call which is a dead giveaway that you a blue box. If the phone company is alert you will be na. when they check their billing tapes. Never use long distance information from a home phone. Your security should never depend on someone else's stupidity.

Here are the credit cards for two of those companies producing 2600 detectors.

You are cordially invited to the 2nd annual international Phone Phreaks' Convention

SEPT. 8, 1973

10 a.m. - 5 p.m.

$4.00 contribution, YIPL subscribers free

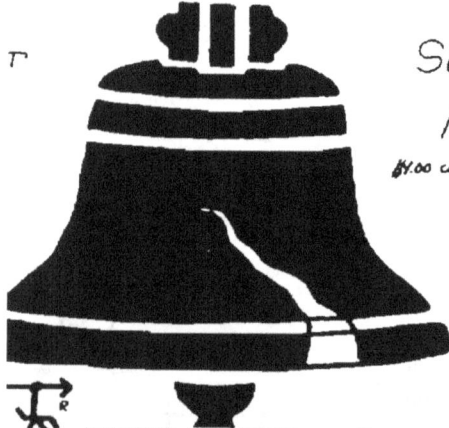

BE SURE AND BRING AN ISSUE OF YIPL ADDRESSED TO YOU FOR FREE CONVENTION ADMISSION.

Northeast Electronics   Teltronics
Concord, N. H.   Lakeland, Fla.
224-6511-004U (603 Area) 683-7409-531Z (813 Area)

It's reasonable to assume that these people will only supply independent companies. The Bell system has designed its own. It's been known for some time that Bell has had a few 2600 detectors that recorded the MF numbers. These are probably used when they suspect a blue box is being used from a home phone and want to gather evidence for prosecution. According to Bell security, the computor program which processes the billing tapes now looks for 800 calls longer that 10 minutes as well as an excessive number of 800 calls.

-Alex, U.S.-

Phone operator tells of Ma Bell's "Watergate"

To the Editor:

I work as a telephone operator in New York City, handling "Directory Assistance" (411) calls. Last year, during the election campaign, we saw our boss, N.Y. Telephone (AT&T) pull off its own Watergate-type undercover action against the Democratic Party.

The Democrats had set up a fund-raising "telethon" during the campaign, with the idea that people would call up and pledge donations. We were not allowed to give out this number! Our supervisors received a written memo from higher management, which laid down this procedure:" ...If a customer calls asking for the Democratic Party telethon number, instruct the operator to say, "I'm sorry, I have no listing. . ." Only if the customer becomes insistent, instruct the operator to transfer the call to a supervisor, who will, if necessary, give the number."

There's an expression that's very popular among telephone company management. It goes, "One hand washes the other." AT&T probably did a whole lot more to help Nixon that we don't even know about. One thing we know that Nixon did though, he slapped us with the wage-freeze one day before our last contract ran out!

(name withheld)
Brooklyn, N. Y.

Dear YIPL:

Here's a way to beat the high cost of living.
1. Steal an adjustable price marker from a supermarket. It has about 5 wheels that turn to whatever price you want.
2. Go to your local hobby shop and buy a small tube of Methyl Ethyl Ketone, "MEK", a resin catalyst.
You are now ready to fight dat ole debbil inflation. You've got your pricer, your MEK, and some paper tissue. Now go to the store. Stick to canned foods at first. Find what you want. Put a drop of MEK on the price. Wait a second, then wipe it off with your paper tissue. Select the price you want(between 10 and 25 cents less than the store price) on your pricer, and stamp away. If they question the price at the checkout, get abusive. Call them money grubbing bloodsuckers and threaten to call the price commission. They will not bother you again. Bon appetite and good luck.
-Stainless, R. L.-

YIPL-

To get the phone to ring in Denver, dial 6191, then hang up. It will ring one long continuous ring until you pick it up. The 660 thing suggested in #18 doesn't work.
Question- what is the point of driving the Nashville info. ops crazy, as suggested by one of the letters in #18? They are just as oppressed by Pa Bell as the rest of us, and certainly not responsible for the way we are ripped-off. I think its important to remember that the phone co's lackeys are poor and starving like us, probably hate the phone co. as much as we do, and also are being exploited by it. They aren't the enemy, and I'm sure they have enough problems(like maintaining their sanity in a job like that) without being unneccesarily hassled. end of diatribe
-Nancy, Denver-

Dear YIPL;

You may be interested to know that, according to the little booklets 'Pa Bell' sends out to its stockholders, a phone call from a pay-phone costs them 7 1/2¢. This includes buying their equipment from Western Electric (whom they own switch, hook and dial). That means they get 2 1/2¢ as free money. Also, at the end of '72, Bell owned over 105 million of the world's 300 million and the U.S.'s 128 million. There are also 1800 independent Telcos to divide what's left.

-P. A. , Tucson-

How to get out of paying deposit:
Feel Free! to lie to phone co. They don't have time to check your answers, especially in spring and fall in college towns. When they ask, "Are you married?' say YES. When they ask where you work, NEVER say, "I'm a student." Tell them you're civil service. When they ask, "Do you have a bank account?" say YES and mention checking account in one local bank and a savings account in another. When they ask, "How long have you been at that address?" say a year and name your landlord. If they still want a deposit, get very insulted and say "To hell with it." Then apologize: "Gee, I'm not mad at you personally, but those stupid company policies! I'll bet working there is a real drag." Call 2 or 3 days later, go thru the above routine again, & you probably will get the phone with no hassle about a required deposit. Very important-After several months, often 6, you are entitled to your deposit back. The phone company will give you interest on the deposit in the form of phone credit, but it's no bargain. The interest can be earned at any bank, but the phone company invests your money in ways to make a fortune for them and much less for you. Don't let them use your money! If you have your friends do this it will mean less money to spend on Western Electric's defense contracts. They were the bloodsuckers behind the ABM.

The phone company also invests money from phone bills and the sooner they get it, the more profits they get. Don't ever send in your bill until the last possible day marked on the bill.
Be sure to call these swell people at convenient times. Area code is 606.
Honeywell...299-0449- Ask them about contract DAAA-21-73-CO286 of January 1973. And ask them about the $30.9 million Navy contract for the Rockeye II cluster bomb. Ask them why they keep working for a company that makes 40% of its profits from anti-personnel weapons.

-M. T., Kentucky-

STUCK STACKS?

A memo from the Director of Switching Engineering to the various Bell Engineers reveals that a device has be built to prevent stacked tandems. It is being installed in all senders with varying degrees of haste. We have some copies of the memo in Destructory Assistance.

Dear YIPL,
While on the phone with a friend, I heard clicks on the line. Then an operator came in and told me that there was another party trying to reach me and that it was an emergency. I heard the clicks a long time and when I asked her why she was listening in so long she told me she was trying to find out if my conversation was important enough to break into. And when I asked her her name, she hung up.
-RK, NY-

Hot News Item! In issue 11 we stated that the Black Box is primarily for long-distance calls, and that local calls may be disconnected if the switch is not immediately switched to "Free". Tests in several areas of New York show that local calls will not be disconnected and will be free! Calls from a pay phone will also be free. There are reports that certain areas will disconnect local calls automatically in 10 to 30 seconds, but often the phone is picked up and hung up too slowly, thus accounting for the disconnection. If the procedure is done within 1/2 second, no disconnection will occur, unless the local phone system is so designed. Highest safety will be afforded when calls are kept under 3 minutes.

GENERAL TELEPHONERS!

We now have a fact sheet identical to our issue 11-Receiving Long Distance calls that is for readers served by GenTel, which uses Automatic Electric phones, not Western Electric. State clearly that you live in a GenTel area when writing us.

Published for informational purposes only by the Youth International Party Line.

BE SURE AND BRING AN ISSUE OF YIPL ADDRESSED TO YOU FOR FREE CONVENTION ADMISSION.

BOOKS
Steal This Book $2.25
Monopoly $1.20

20

FROM: YIPL, Room 504, 152 W. 42 St., N. Y., N. Y. 10036

CALLS GONG UP! It's just a question of time before the 10-cent telephone call becomes history. And very little time at that.
Starting May 1 the cost of a telephone call in the state of Washington rose to 15 cents, making Washington the first state in the Bell System to abandon the 10-cent call.
The Bell System has on file a request to raise all local calls to 20 cents each in the following states: New York, Florida, Maryland, Indiana and Oregon. PARADE • MAY 27, 1973

TAP

no. 21

TECHNOLOGICAL AMERICAN PARTY

august-september 1973

No fancy excuses: We changed our name because we want people to know where we really are and what we hope to become. Technological American Party is rapidly becoming a people's warehouse of technological information, and a name like Youth International Party Line simply didn't ring a bell, even if you were trying to find out how to contact the phone phreaks, except of course for the Party Line. We've been receiving so much information lately about gas and electric meters, locks, even chemistry, that a name change is definitely in order. We seriously doubt that phones will cease to be our main interest, but it really isn't fair to ignore the rest of what science has to offer us.

Because so much varied information will begin to be covered and researched, the newsletter will try to mainly cover items of the most general interest, as it always has. In addition, we will start preparing more reprints of the "fact sheet" type, so that those of you who desire certain areas of info can get it.

What we need is for YOU to contribute ideas. We want to know what you know, and what you want to know. Any field, and we mean anything, that would be difficult or impossible to learn about is a likely candidate. This means that, as usual, we will be covering information about subjects that happen to be illegal as well as legal activities. Naturally, we don't advocate performing illegal activities, though our readers sometimes do. There is a question as to whether a free society can even ban advocacy of illegal activities, but our policy of disclaiming the stuff comes from a belief that telling people what to do is like telling them what they can't do.

All of our information comes from readers. If you don't help your fellow readers, we'll have to put out blank issues. So start opening up other fields, such as the ones mentioned above and anything else that you think needs researching and distributing. Remember- TAP is an equal opportunity destroyer.

NEW RATES !!

Back Issues are 50¢ each.
Subscriptions - 10 issues - US Bulk rate $5.
US First Class in plain sealed envelope $7.
Canada & Mexico First Class $7.
Foreign $8.
IMPORTANT! Include mailing label or Xerox copy when writing to TAP about your subscription.
Book - Monopoly $1.20.
Electronic Courses - 50¢ each A - DC Basics,
B - AC Basics, C - Phone Basics, D - Amplifiers.
TAP T-shirts $4. Specify size: Small, Med., Large, X-Large.
Send only check or money order (No Cash) to
TAP, Room 418, 152 West 42 Street, New York, N.Y. 10036
This is a mail drip only.
OFFICE: 1201 Broadway, Room 608, New York, N.Y. 10021
HOURS: WEDNESDAY, 6 - 9 pm.

HELP IS NEEDED

Please send all available information relating to the subjects listed below for an upcoming article:

Toll Fraud Detectors- especially Black Box detectors(one made by Hekiman Laboratories, 2351 Shady Grove Rd., Rockville, Md. 20850.)We have all Teltronics literature.

Free Electricity and Gas-include pictures of the meters and feed lines in your area and methods used.

Directory of Alternative Society Projects 1973. 250 pages packed with information, free schools, communes, alternative technology, etc. plus freakier schemes like fucking schools, how to make 25,000 pounds growing dope & how to abolish the money system. Order through your library or for ₤1 from BIT information & help service, 146 Great Western Rd., London W. 11 (tel. KP182ST, KP0442298219ST) The Underground Press Syndicate member list is available free(self-addressed, stamped envelope) from UPS, Box26, Village Sta., NY, NY 10014. (212 242-3888). The Best way to keep up with what YIP is doing is to subscribe($3 or free if broke) to YIPSTER TIMES, Box 384, Staten Island, NY 10302 (212-477-6243).

DEFENSE FUND

As you probably have heard, Abbie's been busted for allegedly selling cocaine to some agents, and the D.A. has made it pretty clear that this isn't just another bust. It's to put Abbie away for life and make a spectacle of him. He and the other defendants intend to challenge the laws classifying cocaine with heroin and they're going to need money to do it. We know most people think Abbie has a lot of money, but he's almost broke. It took 4 weeks to raise bail.

TAP readers have a lot to be grateful to Abbie for. Without him this newsletter wouldn't exist. Aside from giving away over $100,000 from book sales to political groups, Abbie has donated time and money to this newsletter, with no intention of it being an ego booster or the source of a future defense fund. We should return the favor and help him out. Let's let him know that TAP readers support him. Send whatever you and your friends can afford to Abbie Hoffman & Friends Legal Defense, c/o Gerald Lefcourt(Abbie's lawyer), 640 Broadway, N.Y., N.Y. 10012. If you can, try to let others know about the legal fund so they can help, too. Thanks. If all you can afford to send is a buck, please do it.

CONVENTION

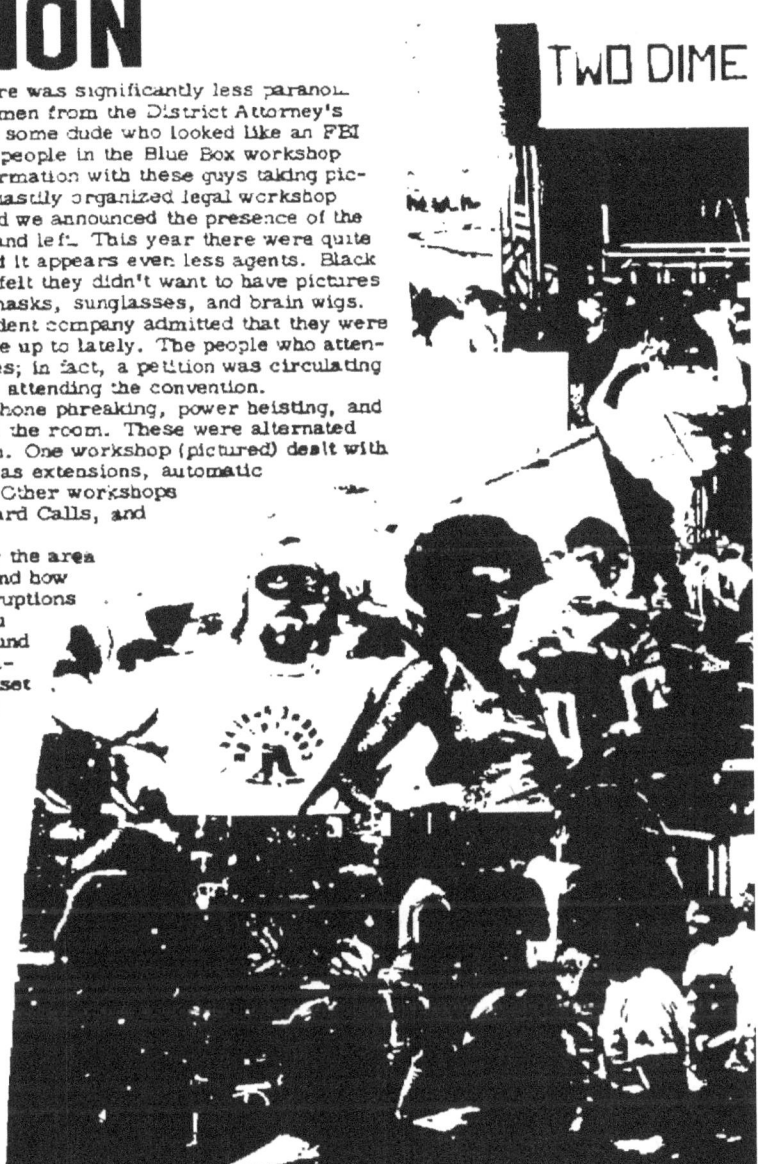

TWO DIME

We had a lot of fun at this year's convention. There was significantly less paranoia than at last year's Convention. At that time, two men from the District Attorney's office, two men from the telephone company, and some dude who looked like an FBI agent posing as a reporter were really giving the people in the Blue Box workshop the creeps. Everybody was afraid to give out information with these guys taking pictures and making recordings at the workshop. A hastily organized legal workshop with Abbie helped to put things in perspective, and we announced the presence of the phone company agents, who promptly got uptight and left. This year there were quite a few more people attending (several hundred) and it appears even less agents. Black masks were handed out at the door for those who felt they didn't want to have pictures taken. Some people came already equipped with masks, sunglasses, and brain wigs. A pair of security men from a Rochester Independent company admitted that they were only there on their own, but to learn what we were up to lately. The people who attended felt little animosity toward the few agent-types; in fact, a petition was circulating urging that all agents be paid double overtime for attending the convention.

Eight half-hour videotapes on many phases of phone phreaking, power heisting, and using slugs were shown on video monitors around the room. These were alternated with workshops in four areas around the ballroom. One workshop (pictured) dealt with installing extra devices on your phone line, such as extensions, automatic answering equiptment, hold buttons and the like. Other workshops dealt with Con Ed, Boxes of all colors, Credit Card Calls, and "reforming" the phone company.

A number of display boxes were scattered over the area One demonstrated the busy tones and dial tones and how they are generated and timed to 60 and 120 interruptions per minute. Another played interesting things you might hear should you be so fortunate to call around the world to different phone numbers, like Dial-a-Disc in France, weather in Tokyo, or Sex on Sunset Strip. There was a display that demonstrated the 2600 cycle whistle and allowed you to practice it into a telephone handset, and probably the most popular was a Red Box, in which you could hear what each of the main circuits did and how the actual Coin Denomination Tones are produced. Some people were even making cassette recordings from the Red Box display unit!

The press was there in force, filming and interviewing anyone they could get to talk. The atmosphere seemed very light and people did seem to be enjoying the afternoon. Back issues were being sold rapidly, and most people passed up the organic carob cake and brownies in order to watch the videotapes or attend the workshops.

Al Bell gave a short speech on how the phone company plans to raise the public phone rate to 20¢ and blame the increased cost on phone phreaks. A walking pay phone was making the rounds, soliciting 20¢ contributions here and there. Some attendees were circulating credit card lists and back issues of Telephony.

The display boxes were built especially for the convention and we knew that people would want to know how they were constructed. The 2600 cycle whistle detector is actually a toll-fraud detector since it activates upon hearing 2600. We had some schematics at the convention but seeing as they were free, they were all gone by noon. If you would like schematics for the 2600 cycle detector, the displayed red box, and the dual-tone oscillator(which is not, by the way, a blue box), we have more of them in and we're asking 15¢ each(free if you can't afford it). They use transistors and IC's in each of them and each circuit can be built for about $15. If you received a circuit, be sure and note the correction on the Red Box sheet. For the price of a SELF-ADDRESSED STAMPED ENVELOPE you can also get a copy of the Convention Schedule which includes Joe Engressia's and Captain Crunch's telephone numbers in case you want to rap with them. We have also compiled a list of typical Destructory Assistance topics which is free if you send the envelope as above.

If you attended the convention, give feedback. What didn't you like? What do you wish there was but wasn't? What, if anything, did you like? Got any ideas on the next convention? Let us know!

We're working hard to get more Phone Phreak Convention T-shirts and others. We'll let you know next issue. Meanwhile, help recruit friends and Telco employees as researchers and contributors to TAP. If you want to do research, tell us!

CORRECTION

CHANGE THIS:

TO THIS:

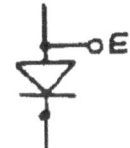

DISPLAYED RED BOX

AUTOMATIC PHONE TAP

This tap is a device which records directly from a telephone line all conversations on that line. It con-sists of 3 parts:
1. An ordinary dial phone equipped with a "monitor" switch. (Or a mute box, black box, or issue #11)
2. A tape recorder.
3. A line relay.
A monitor switch can be installed quite easily. All you need is a screwdriver, a Single-pole, single-throw toggle switch and some electrical tape. Remove the cover from the phone, disconnect the green wire from the "RR" terminal and wrap one switch wire and the green wire together with a piece of tape.. The other switch wire is wrapped around the "RR" screw and tightened. One position of the switch will give you a dial tone. This is the "Normal" position. The other position of the switch will let you hear your phone line without getting a dial tone. This is the same as the "Free" position in Issue #11. Next you need a line relay that will be used to turn on a tape recorder when the phone is being used. Parts: A 1/2 watt, 10,000 ohm resistor (10¢) and a sensitive, low voltage relay, Lafayette Radio #99P60915 @ $2.57 + .43 postage (Lafayette, 111 Jericho Tpke, Syosset, NY 11791.) When the relay is con-nected to the phone line(red and green wires) that is not in use (on hook) the relay will be activated thereby open-ing the circuit to the recorder, turning it off. When a phone is picked up, the voltage on the line drops, causing the relay to de-activate, thereby closing the N.C. circuit and turning on the recorder. Things to look for when choosing a recorder are: Cost, Size(small as possible for hiding the tap), Automatic Level Control, Automatic end-of-tape shutoff, and a remote on-off switch (usually in mike). The G.E. M8430 cassette recorder meets all the above for $20.00 at most discount stores. Get a 120 minute tape, and a telephone pickup coil that goes on the handset. To Tap a Line: 1. Hook up a telephone with a monitor switch (on "Free") to the desired line. 2. Hook the line relay up to the same two wires. 3. Switch the phone to "monitor" ("Free"). 4. Remove the handset. 5. Slip the pick-up coil onto the handset (the receiver) and plug it into the mike jack on the recorder. 6. Hook the recorder's remote on-off switch to the N.C. contacts of the line relay. With the GE M8430, a convenient sub-mini jack can be used. 7. Switch Tape recorder to Record. Now when a phone is picked up, the relay will turn on the tape recorder, which will record everything to be heard on the monitor phone. Don't get caught!

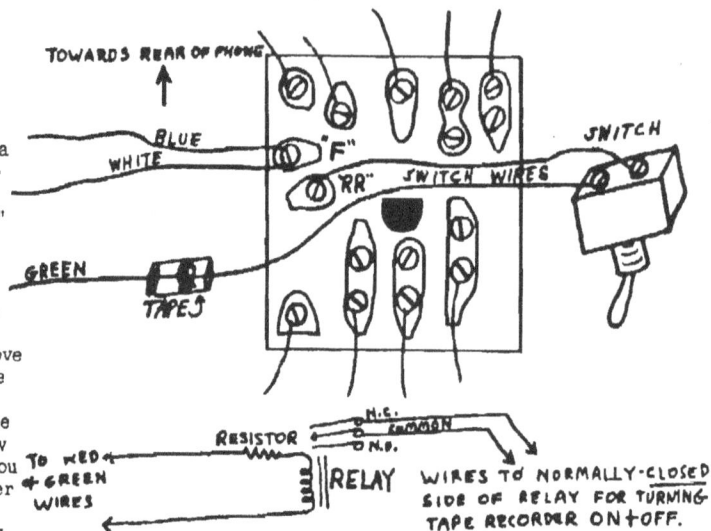

Jury indicts president of phone firm

SEATTLE (AP) — David J. Henny, president of the Whidbey Telephone Co., has been indicted by the federal grand jury on charges of fraud.

The panel returned an in-dictment Tuesday charging Henny, 43, with eight counts of wire fraud and two counts of intercepting phone calls from customers.

It accuses Henny of devis-ing schemes to defraud Gen-eral Telephone Co., Pacific Northwest Bell and the par-ent firm, American Tele-phone and Telegraph Co., of more than $100,000.

Conviction on all charges could result in a maximum sentence of 50 years in pris-on and $28,000 in fines.

A report on the case was carried in a copyrighted arti-cle Wednesday by the Seattle Post-Intelligencer.

The charges concern the billing system used by inde-pendent telephone companies for calls placed through the lines of larger firms. Under the arrangement, the inde-pendent firm pays the large company the revenue for each call of less than three minutes but gets a larger amount back from the larger company.

The indictment claims that Henny inflated the number of calls "in order to obtain by fraud" a higher share of the revenue than was owed to his firm.

The government also con-tends that Henny set up an arrangement through the Whidbey telephone exchange which permitted his em-ployes to make toll-free long distance calls.

BEGINNERS ONLY!

You can now learn about Electronics easily and quickly with our new Correspondence Course. The first one is on Basic Electrical Concepts and includes a few TAP-type projects and easy-to-read explana-tions of electricity. By reading this and others com-ing out each month you'll learn how to build any of the projects that have been printed by us in the past. You'll learn how to read schematics, buy parts and materials cheap, safety, etc. You can no longer say that what we publish is above your head because any beginner can learn from these courses. Women are especially urged to take the course as they usually have a fear of electronic concepts and this course will be understood by all. Let's hear from you! It's like a back issue and is 50¢, and free if you can't afford it(let us know).

TAP, ROOM 418, 152 W. 42 ST., N.Y. N.Y. 10036

TAP

THE NEWSLETTER THAT ADVOCATES "VIOLENCE"

BUILD THE ANSWEROO

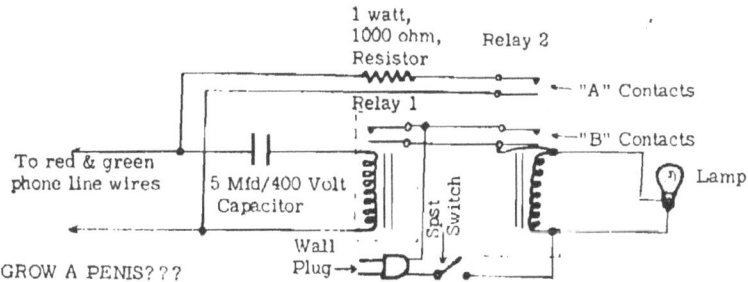

1 watt, 1000 ohm, Resistor

Relay 2

"A" Contacts

Relay 1

"B" Contacts

To red & green phone line wires

5 Mfd/400 Volt Capacitor

Lamp

Spst Switch

Wall Plug→

SPIRO AGNEW- is it really an anagram-GROW A PENIS???
-CCR-

TAP D.A.

Destructory Assistance has a new list of subjects out, which you can find out about by sending us info on that or another subject. If you don't have info to trade, don't worry, we edit and condense the material and put it in TAP. To trade info with DA, just send us a stamped, self-addressed envelope large enough to hold the info you want, which we'll try to find for you. Wait a couple of weeks for us to dig the stuff out of our files. We've got different schematics for blue and black boxes, articles on bugs, a copy of the Bell memo on tandem stacking, newspaper articles on phone phreaks, Free electric and gas meters, and lots more. This is TAP's major source of info so please help us out.   Our list of subjects is free with an envelope as above. And if computers is your thing, write to HEAD CRASH- DA's computer password and information exchange to trade info.

And if you're a computer novice, write for Head Crash's new Beginner's Course on Computers (50¢). More Head Crash Courses will be available soon.

NEW RATES !!

Back Issues are 50¢ each.
Subscriptions - 10 issues - US Bulk rate $5.
US First Class in plain sealed envelope $7.
Canada & Mexico First Class $7.
Foreign $8.
IMPORTANT! Include mailing label or Xerox copy when writing to TAP about your subscription.
Book - Monopoly $1.20.
Electronic Courses - 50¢ each A - DC Basics,
B - AC Basics, C - Phone Basics, D - Amplifiers.
TAP T-shirts $4. Specify size: Small, Med., Large, X-Large.
Send only check or money order (No Cash) to
TAP, Room 418, 152 West 42 Street, New York, N.Y. 10036
This is a mail drop only.
OFFICE: 1201 Broadway, Room 608, New York, N.Y. 10001
HOURS: WEDNESDAY, 6 - 9 pm.

The Answeroo is a handy device offered by no one (yet) that answers your phone before it rings. This is especially useful to lovers who live in their parent's homes and like to call each other late at night. Instead of the phones in the house ringing, a light or other appliance (radio, TV, etc.) comes on. You can then go to the phone, turn off the Answeroo, and talk.

Relay 1 is the Line Relay(Issue #17). When the phone rings, it sends current to Relay 2 and the light. Contacts "B" lock Relay 2 on, and Contacts "A" put the phone on hold(not free). Using a 56 volt zener diode in place of the 1000 ohm resistor would give a "free" hold until you answered the phone, unless you then answer with a Black Box(Issue #11). The single-pole, single-throw on-off switch, two 115 volt AC relays (one of them should be double-pole, the other single-pole, for relays 2 & 1 respectively), the 5 mfd. non-polar capacitor (200 volts or more), and a resistor are all you need. Cost-under $15. Have fun!

HELP IS NEEDED

We need more information on the following topics for upcoming articles in TAP.

Toll Fraud Detectors and Detection Methods, and especially Black Box detectors(Hekiman Labs). We already have Teltronics info.

Getting Free Gas and Electricity -IMPORTANT- if you know anything about it please write in quick!

Magnets- We'd like to know all esoteric uses for magnets that you know of.

DEFENSE FUND

Please send whatever you can afford to prevent Abbie and his friends from being sent to jail for life (no parole for 15 Years), because cocaine is classified as heroin (though it is non-addictive and shunned by junkies). Send your support to Abbie Hoffman & Friends Legal Defense, 640 Broadway, N.Y.,N.Y. 10012. Please don't send cash. Thanks.

Hi-
This may end some of the confusion about the number to call which gives you a computer-generated voice telling you your phone number. In NYC there are 4 numbers-They are:730, 840, 958, 880. One will always work(except in a few C. O. s) The numbers rotate each month. Other boros may lead or lag 1 month. List is for 1973 but I think it will be same next year.
-FLH, NY-

TAP-
You might tell Phellow Phreaks in NYC that there are three different 3-digit numbers to dial for finding out the number you're calling from, and that they are regional. What's more, Pa Bell likes to switch 'em now & then to confuse us. That's the reason(they're regional) that one might work for one area but not another. They are: 958, 311, and 221. If N. Y. C. telephone subscribers have suspected that the number of "additional message units" they're being charged for on their monthly bill is too high, it's probably true. I got it on good authority (a former operator) that NY Tel routinely overcharges customers on additional m. u. 's every month. And they get away with it since message units are not verifiable, because they are not itemized like toll calls. You have to take their word. The padding takes place not in the computers but in Accounting, where Pa Bell's hard-working CPA's are under orders to pile on a heap of extra message units because who'll be the wiser? And when one complains to the B. O. Rep. that he keeps track of his calls and couldn't possibly have made so many, we're told that they will"check our equipment"-a ruse, a diversionary tactic, because that's not where the skullduggery is being done. Get it?
-H. R. Holdafone-

Dear TAP,
There existed among the gang back in Vancouver some very sick minds who delighted in setting various parts of a payphone on fire. What they would do is open the phone book up around the middle, pour gasoline on same, placed a paper cup containing a particular mixture in it upon the soaked book and walk away. In about two min-utes, the book would be aflame and would parboil the plastic handset into submission and if the booth itself was molded out of plastic, a cheerful blaze greeted the pigs and other such carbon compaounds. The mix-ture in the cup was about half a heaping teaspoon of Potassium Permanganate(chemical and hobby stores) and, to be added just before an innocent departure, one drop of glycerine(drugstores for ointment use). This pile of goodies usually erupts into a white hot flare capable of igniting almost anything, including gas fumes. The reaction, by the way, takes from 30 seconds on a hot day with finely ground Pot Per to 6 minutes on a cold day with clunky Compound P. Also ideal for quiet little garbage cans at school or maybe even Telco vehicle's gas tank in a small bag-gie or a gas sodden piece of construction that you feel is bad for the environment or simply remote & safe ignition of fireworks. Fagen Das Telefunken Ges-ellschaft!! Freundlichst,
-BW, MANITOBA-

We have some inexpensive instructional plan sheets for the display models featured at the Convention. The 2600 whistle perfector is a 2600 detector similar to existing toll-fraud detectors. The Displayed Red Box is similar to Issue #16's circuit with an improved IC timer, LED lights to demonstrate operation, and a few other improvements. The circuit can be used as a portable with a few changes we explain, and is far more reliable than the older circuit. The Dual Tone Oscillator is a circuit for demonstrating signalling tones, and can even be used as a simple blue box. The sheets are 15¢ each(free if you can't afford it). We also have copies of the Convention schedule(free), including Cap'n Crunch's and Joe Engressia's #'s.

Dear TAP,
When using a blue box to call any country which is on the IDDD list, if it has a 2-digit country code you can leave off the zero from in front of the country code once you have obtained a register(i. e. -KP61 2 2074 ST instead of KP081 2 2074). It will be treated as a cust-omer-dialed call, which means you won't be able to reach the inward or other operators. If it is a 3-digit country code then it will be automatically treated as a customer-dialed call unless you use a special "op-erator country code" which starts with 0 & has no re-lation to the regular C. C.
-H. GORDON LIDDY, NY-

To Destructory Assistance-
Two IOTC accessable areas are 202 and 713. Any WATS number such as 800-392-XXXX or 800-424-XXXX to these areas will work. Also 800-447-XXXX. (IOTC means you can box KP 011 country code ST and you'll be automatically routed to the correct 18- sender).Is there a direct route to Moscow off of the 182 sender?(White Plains) I've been get-ting some overseas point by dialing KP182ST, KP171121ST. It's usually a busy signal (distant) and when I call Japan and ask for Moscow she says it's too early in the morning and they don't answer.
  Dial KP713 141ST or KP202 141ST and ask for"overseas routing for Paris ,France please", or whatever. Ask for IOTC. She'll give you all the routing instructions(ignore "Mark XXX..."). Call KP713 151ST. It's called '1st at-tempt failure desk" and it will record everything you say to it. Play a radio newscast for them or talk about phone phreaking.
-SW, TEXAS-

NOTE: You can reach a Moscow Test Center by using overseas sender KP188ST, (although it's supposed to be served by NY4, 183) or IOTC KP011 071ST, then KP071 095 080ST, when the trunk chirps play KP01 6ST. A Moscow test board will answer. They often speak some foriegn languages(including some poor English). Also, try Israel, 972, or just 72. Here are some cities:
2-Jerusalem 53-38378-Tul Karem 65-23854-Genin
3-Tel Aviv 53-38373-Nablus   2-97-Hebron
4-Haifa   59-Elat   2-922610-Auja
53-Natania 65-Afula ,Nazareth

Dear TAP,

Did you know the restricted line feature of many Centrex installations can be bypassed? One may usually call outside by dialing 9 for an external dial tone and then dialing the number, provided that it lies in the local area. If more than 7 digits are dialed a recording comes on. But this may be bypassed by dialing 9 then 0 followed immediately by the first digit of the # then complete dialing of the number without the area code. When the assistance operator comes on insist that you have been having difficulty, reaching the local number even though you've been dialing the area code. Then you ask her to try the number for you, billing it to a credit card or the centrex line. This info should be very useful.

                                        -JA, NY-

Dear TAP,

Toll restrictors are usually used at motels that have direct dial out type phones. A typical one will say " Dial 8 for local" "Dial 9 for long distance". When you dial 8 or 9 you will get another dial tone and then you can proceed to dial your own local number. Some phones you can dial info and/or 800 without the operator coming on the line but these are rare and on most types, the operator comes on the line and makes your call. The toll restrictor will not allow you to dial "1" in order to make your own long distance calls. However several of these restrictors only protect the first and second digits and can be beat in the following way... Dial the one digit shown on the phone to make local calls (usually 8) then dial the first two digits of the exchange you're in plus the digit 1 and you will find a new dial tone and the world at your fingertips. You may dial direct and the motel line is charged for the call, or you may use your favorite box without worry, assuming you have used another name at the register.

                                        -Sparky-

Dear TAP,

I am an electronics technician by trade and a past employee of Pa Bell and Johnny General. I have been a phreak since 1958 when I made my first free call.

The resistance of the ringers is not the factor measured when friendly test board "bridges" your line. The circuit(basically)that they use is as follows: You will recognize the circuit as a simple ohmmeter, but why is the voltmeter connected in series? I don't know but Pa measures current with it. "100 volts of short" means a dead short on the line. Zero volts, an

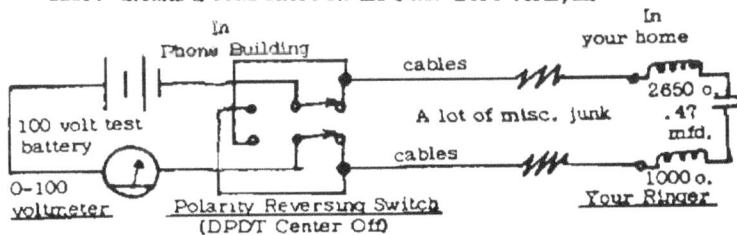

open. Now the important part, the reversing switch. The testboardman flips it back and forth and the bounce of the meter(hook an ordinary ohmmeter to a capacitor and reverse the leads and you'll see the same effect) lets him estimate the # of ringers. Cruddy insulation, temperature, and distance from the C.O. affect readings. A key telephone may look like 3 ringers, etc. Capacitance is most important with the D.C. winding resistance next. At one flip per second, coil inductance is very important, too. As or detecting phones without ringers, Pa Bell can't do it. I have 17 telephones and a key system(I use my own "one bell simulator", 3650ohms and .47 mfd. in series). You can safely connect as many ringerless phones as you like. Peace be with you on the tandems forever(ka-chirp).

                              -Almon B. Strowger, CA.-

NOTE: Connecting extra extensions is in issue #1.

HOW WE CATCH RED BOXERS

by Milton Moritz, United Telephone System

I personally view the red box as a much less dangerous item to us than the blue box. The basis for this is as follows:

1. The red box does not work on all pay phones. The electronic tones which it produces match those of the new "single slot" pay stations. Older pay phones still use the two internal bells to register the coins dropped into the phone.

2. Telephone operators are trained the electronic tones. Our pay stations all produce exactly the same tones. If the red box is slightly out of adjustment, the operator will normally recognize the tone as abnormal and report the call for further inquiry or investigation.

3. Each toll call, whether from a residence phone or pay station, is rated and billed by our computer. The amount of money collected from each pay station is also reported to data processing and a computer printout compares the calls billed to that station against the money collected. When a pay station starts going "short" we immediately check to see if this is electromechanical failure, operator error, data processing problems, internal theft, or external theft. Thieves and cheats are, like the rest of us(our emphasis), creatures of habit, and their activities will form a pattern in a fairly brief period of time. "

Security Letter is an anti-ripoff newsletter for corporations that is itself a ripoff at $48/yr., and who attended our convention last year without permission to rip us off and report on the convention in Telephony. Ed. Robert McCrie's latest issue, we're told, rips off part of Ron Rosenbaum's excellent article from the Village Voice on our second convention. If you happen to be receiving SL, you're wasting your money. The articles are a waste and filled with (stolen)errors. anyway.-TAP.

Dear TAP,

In a past issue, you told us about Security Letter, and I sent off for a subscription. Why the fuck didn't you people tell me that they also charge $48 a year for a subscription to their 4-page deal that comes out every 2 weeks. A little hint about sending telegrams by phone: I sent one to Florida on April 29, and didn't get the bill until September 1. A nice little thing to keep in mind... You mentioned this obliquely in one issue, but I thought I'd clarify it. To get a call for a nickel on a fortress phone: insert a nickel. You will hear a slight change in the background noise. Hold down the hook switch until you hear a very faint click in the handset, about a second. Let up the hookswitch, and you have a dial tone. Unfortunately, the dial will not be connected, so you have to tap out the number on the hookswitch, which takes practice.

                                        -CS, HOUSTON-

Dear Persons,

Under the bank Security Act, passed several years ago, all banks that handle checking accounts must make photo copies of all cancelled checks and keep microfilm records in their central records dept. These copies can be inspected on demand by Treasury Dept. agents, without any warrants whatsoever. When the Fed snoops get around to harrassing radical libertarians(individualist anarchists) then I'll be under strong possibility that Big Brother is watching my financial transactions. Until then, however, I'm not going to give them a head start over a miniscule 50¢ check to YIPL. (I'm not saying "I don't care until it hits me"). ACLU, Proxmire and others are fighting the Act, but Chairman Patman of the House Banking committe is for it and won't hold hearings on it.

                                        -RE, NY-

NOTE: TAP suggests readers send money orders, which need not contain your real name or address.

Ma Bell's Ripoff Warning

Pacific Telephone Co. displeased over the growing gamesmanship of its customers who deliberately won't put postage stamps on envelopes used to pay their bills, took stern steps yesterday to stop "the eight-cent ripoff."

The company started yesterday mailing warnings to all of its six million customers, telling them to stop the illegal practice — or Ma Bell won't accept their mail.

About 2.3 per cent of the customers — about 135,000 per month — have been leaving the stamps off.

In addition, a phone company spokesman said, the errant customers could face Post Office fines of up to $200 for failing to put stamps on mail "with the intent to avoid payment of lawful postage."

The phone company estimates the practice — growing in popularity in recent months — could cost the telephone company here about $140,000 this year to make good on "postage due" envelopes it receives.

The stiff price of the no-stamp game, company people said, will certainly be passed on to telephone customers.

Here's what the phone company has in store for the customers it describes as "postage offenders":

● The Post Office acting on a phone company complaint, will now intercept all mail to Pacific Telephone that does not have a postage stamp on it:

● If the envelope has a return address, carriers will take it back to the sender, collect eight cents for postage and ten cents for handling and the sender will have to pay another eight cents for a new stamp to mail his bill

● If there is no return address, the Post Office will open the envelope in an effort to locate the sender, and, if it can't, postal officials will destroy the checks or money orders or return them to issuing agencies to stop payment on them.

● If the payment is in cash and there is no return address, the Post Office will eventually turn the money over to its general fund

(used to pay claims on insured mail).

Phone company officials said yesterday that in where the Post Office intercepts mail and is unable to find the sender, the customers will be considered delinquent on their bills.

Since the average household telephone bill in the Bay Area is $15 per month, the phone company officials admit there is some risk to the company treasury in the crackdown.

"We don't think we will lose a substantial amount in the first place," said a spokesman.

"In the second place, we believe our warning will solve the problem."

Pacific Telephone, estimating a 30 per cent increase this year in the no-stamp practice, is not alone, of course, in the field.

Other utilities — especially Pacific Gas and Electric Co. — along with banks, insurance and oil companies and big department stores all get caught with postage-due messages from their most loyal customers.

Nothing mentioned about many _EMPTY_ (or stuffed with bill envelopes folded). Ha!
-CALIFORNIA-

CORRECTION

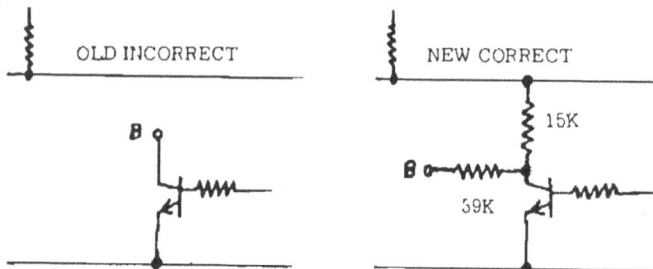

OLD INCORRECT   NEW CORRECT

One more correction to the Displayed Red Box sheet.

Published for informational purposes only by the Technological American Party.

TAP, ROOM 418, 152 W. 42 ST., N.Y. N.Y. 10036

22

Dear TAP,

Bell's PR dept. has free films available on various topics such as TASI, ESS, EDDD. Call up telco business office, and say you would like to find out about renting phone co. educational films. Put on your best Sunday School voice, and tell them that you're in charge of programming for your church youth group (that's how I found out). If they ask what church, have a name ready. They have a nice brochure, and some of the films are very informative.

Have you ever mentioned the fact that out-of-city phone books can be obtained free from Pa? Just call the business office and say you want to get a phone book for another city. They'll switch you to the rep. for your exchange. Give her the info, and she'll(or he'll) get your name & address. If they ask why you want it, just say that you've just moved from there and have a lot of friends there. When they ask if it's a business or residence, say residence(they charge businesses more).

Dear TAP,

Just thought you might be interested in a few pieces of information. First of all, a guy named Dial has invented a lie detector that can be used over the phone. Fun, huh? It measures the stress in a person's voice. He also said that he had sold them to P. D. 's, Gov't. agencies and Big Corporations! What corporation has more voices to deal with and is larger than our friend Pa? Don't get stressed when calling! Right!

For you bugged phreaks, Samuel Line, Jr., Vice-President of a Bell subsidary in Penn., says, "We have been historically against wire-tapping". However, Bell provides a line to the FBI if needed directly from the tapee's home.

You can beat the simplest type of bug (A transmitter in the phone's microphone) by ripping a new mic.off from some other phone and replacing your transmitter with it. If you bang a payphone long enough, the mic. will loosen up. Keep up the good work.

-P, ARIZONA-

TECHNOLOGICAL AMERICAN PARTY

The Energy Crisis was finally spotlighted this month by the Pres to the American Public. It was "suggested" to the people that cutting down highway speeds, shortening school hours (good news in some respects), turning off your home and office lights when unneeded, and lowering the thermostat would give us a savings of considerable magnitude on fuel consumption. The second part of project Independence would be to develop within this country a source of energy which would free us from "reliance on a foriegn enemy... er, energy"...

It seems that this country can only be moved ahead in times of crisis, so instead of preventative structuring of our life systems we get problematic solutions. That is to say we do not really rid ourselves of the disease, we only change its name and place and again wait for a crisis.

Take for instance Gas consumption. A better way to take the same amount of fuel and stretch its potential use would be to expend scientific skills in the developement of a gasoline engine with better mileage. Almost all the American car manufacturers have reduced amounts of miles per gallon this year in their cars. And why not? Along with the ll interests they stand only to win.

The Pres also said cars usually only have one person in them. Anyone who's stood out on the road for hours, freezing their ass off could have told us that. Us hitch-hikers are probably going to be blamed for the high speeds that frightened motorists travel at (the same mentality that blames phone phreaks for rising phone rates). We know that the American People are being fed advertisements that make us CONSUME. But you didn't really expect Pres to get up there and admit that our entire economy (that means his friends' profits) depends upon a continuous increase in CONSUMPTION, which is what caused the whole mess. Buy, Buy, Buy, Throw Away, Throw Away, Oops, better conserve, we'll raise our prices so don't worry!

The same could be said for all gas appliances, and even manufacturers of electric lights. Couldn't a low consumption high-brightness bulb be immediately produced? You bet your blue box! But the most recent trend among the Science communities is to use their abilities in developing either weapons of destruction, or useless niceities like better floor wax, instant cheese dip or pocket calculators (for adding up all your purchases). Let's pray that before we start unrestricted strip mining and other rapings we can get maximum output from already existing fuels and decrease our consumption by using decent mass transit & sharing with others. Three color TV's per family! Now is the time for Bell Labs to come forward and tell us what the fuck they've been puttering around with that would help us instead of lowering AT&Ts construction costs and boosting profits.

The Electric and Gas companies are huge monopolies who have the nerve to sell us the Sun's energy. They have free reign over their rates they charge, the quality of the smoke we're forced to breathe and the oceans and lakes they conveniently dump their wastes into. And don't forget that they plan to risk all our lives by installing unsafe nuclear power plants in the midst of population centers. We'll probably find out sooner or later of the corruption & payoffs that allow the Atomic Energy Commission to ignore

(Continued)

BELL LABS:
Just what the hell have they been doing since 1953?
(Nat. Geographic Photo)

Bell Solar Battery Uses Silicon to Turn Sunlight into Electricity

BACK ISSUES-50¢

1- Extensions, conference switches
2- Blue Box Story and Abbie on ripoffs
3- Telecommand Story
4- Pay Phone Issue
5- Blue Box 1 ⟩ Now obsolete(Issue 12)
6- Blue Box 2 ⟩
7- Tuning your organ
8- Credit card calls and 1972 code
9- Super Duper Project (See Issue 11)
10-
11- Receiving long distance calls free
12- Blue Box Plans
13- International Calls & Box Plans
14- International Calls & AT&T Papers
15- 1973 Credit Code, T Network
16- Red Box Plans

17- Red Box, Line Relay
18- Call Stopper
19 Snoop Light
20- Cheese Box
21- Automatic Phone Tap
22- Answeroo

FACT SHEETS-25¢

1. New Credit Card Fact Sheet
   (Code and How to do it Safely)
2. Receiving Long Distance Calls Free
   (Gen. Tel. version of Issue 11)
Displayed Red Box - 15¢
2600 Whistle Perfector - 15¢
Dual Tone Oscillator with Interrupter - 15¢
List of Destructory Assistance Topics - Free
Schedule from 2nd Int'l Phreak Convention - Free
To receive Sub, via first class envelope, add $1.50
$4 Subscription approx. 10 issues/yr.
Number on address area indicates first issue sent.
Renew if your address has a 13 or less on it.
TAP, ROOM 504, 152 W. 42 ST., N.Y., N.Y. 10036
Mailing address only, check or money order only, NO CASH!

ANTI-BELL BUTTON- 90¢ 10/$3.90
DESTRUCTORY ASSISTANCE- Free, just send as much info as you want back in a stamped, self-addressed envelope.

Steal This Book - $2.25
Monopoly $1.20

All information is free if you can't afford it.

our health and safety, but in the meantime it's comforting to know that these death machines cost money, and we can cut down their revenue and put it to better purposes.

Power phreaks have been around a long time, but on such a small scale that the companies haven't done much to stop it. That will probably change, but they move like turtles and won't be able to do anything on a large scale for years. By then we'll be ten more steps ahead. Besides, God is on our side.

Pay strict attention to the safety rules. We all know that strict obedience to the rules is the only way to get power anyway. More power to you!

Electricity works on the same basic principle in all types of meters around the country, though the meters may look slightly different. First a word about safety.

You will be working with 110 volts like any normal outlet in your home, but you will be closer to that current than if you were plugging in a toaster. So you must know how to be careful. 110 volts can kill you. TAP guarantees that if you stand in a puddle of water, 110 volts will kill you. The same goes for working with wet or sweaty hands or feet. Remember the bathtub in Goldfinger? When you work on electrical lines, wear gloves. If you are too bummed out by gloves, at least wear rubber-soled shoes. And keep dry! Don't stand on a damp floor! If you use your head and work slowly, keeping safety in mind, you will not get shocked. It may seem like a dangerous expedition but it's actually simple to do and a lot of fun. So locate your electric meter, which is usually found in the basement of apartment buildings, or on the outside of houses, put on your gloves and rubbers and get to work. Stand on a rubber mat if you're standing on dirt or dampness. If your electrical meter is among others and isn't clearly marked for your apartment, have a friend turn all your lights on and off simultaneously and then look for the meter that starts and stops. You can tell the meter is starting by the little rotating wheel in front that turns the gears of the little pointers. When you've located your meter, how about jumping it? That will slow the meter down to a crawl, even if you use a lot of electricity, which of course conservation-minded TAPPERs don't do, nor do they rip off, blah, blah, ... This requires removing the meter. The meter simply pulls out with a little wiggling, but it is oftener than not clamped on tight with a ring of metal, which unscrews with a screwdriver. Sometimes an additional lock is put on the ring, called a rollersmith lock. You can't cut a rollersmith lock, but you can make a "key" for it and take it off. The insert shows how to pick this lock.

Remove the ring by bending it slightly, then grab the meter with both hands and pull it straight out. The meter has prongs which fit into sockets on the wall panel. The electricity flows from one socket, into the meter, and out of the meter into the socket which leads up to your home. Now that the meter is out the electricity is turned off. Now we have many choices open to us. We can:

1— Turn the meter pointers backwards to some point.
2— Break the meter, or jam it up.
3— Bypass the meter with a jumper so the meter doesn't move.
4— Bypass the meter with a thin jumper so the meter moves slower.
5— Turn the electricity on if it had been turned off.

TURNING BACK METER

This involves opening the meter case and moving the little dials with your hand. Often there will be a small wire with a lead seal that you have to break in order to open the case. Just cut it off, they never check anyway. Then unscrew the glass case one-eighth of a turn, and remove the glass, turn the dials, and close it back up. Be sure to move the dials back to an actual number. This is a tricky thing to do, and you also have to make sure that you don't get your meter read with the reading less than it was before. If they see you used negative electricity they may have a few questions for you. Get to know when the meter reader comes, how often and on what dates. After

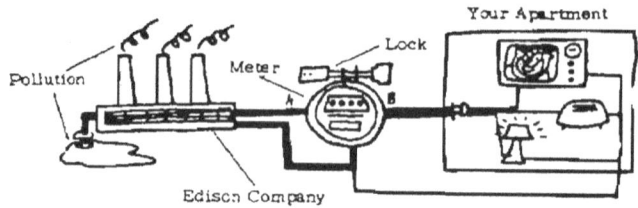

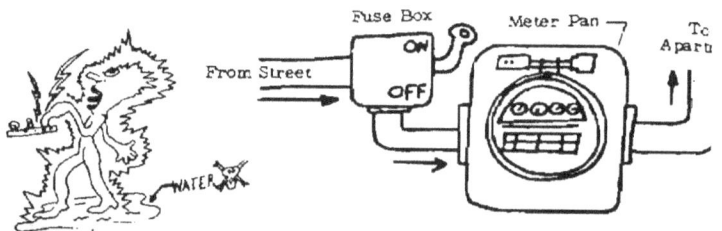

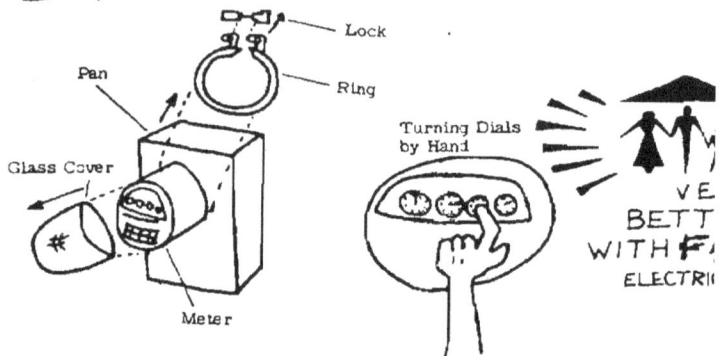

be comes, read the meter, and turn it back to that point right before his next visit. Add a few token kilowatt-hours so they look like you went on a trip and left a clock on. Put the meter, ring, and a little dirt back on to make it look lonely. Be sure to push the meter in straight and firm.

BREAKING OR JAMMING METER

This is dangerous because you can't control it precisely. Rather, you get an anarchistic situation which may result in the meter burning up and the meter reader noticing it. Jamming the meter is accomplished by opening up the case and bending or rusting a few gears to make it stop or to slow down. Stopping the meter isn't recommended because almost everybody's meter is moving continuously and it may look suspicious if your meter is completely dead. But physically jamming the meter usually will stop it completely rather than slow it down. A better way to slow it down is to install a shunt wire inside the meter. We'll show how it's done once we get a few meters from the readers to do research on. Meanwhile you can shunt the meter outside of it's case.

SHUNTING THE METER

If we look at a diagram of how the electricity is fed thru the meter to your home, we see that a jumper wire from point A to point B could carry electricity around the meter. Thus, it would be free. Since the wires in and around the meter are thick, our jumper wire will have to be thick to be able to carry all the electricity, so that none goes thru the meter. A piece of insulated #14 wire will do the trick.

Remove your meter from the meter pan. The back of the meter will have prongs which plug into sockets in the pan. Take a 9" piece of insulated solid copper wire, #14 or #16. Wrap it around the proper terminals, thereby bypassing the meter. In our N.Y. example with a 3-wire Westing-house meter (for places with both 110 and 220 volts), the proper terminals are the two vertically-oriented pairs. There is a horizontal ground terminal; don't connect on to it with the jumpers. The jumpers may have to go to different terminals on other different types of meters, and you can find out the proper terminals with a simple ohm-meter ($4 or less at electronics stores). Since the proper terminals to be shunted already have internal shunts, the ohmmeter will measure less than 1 ohm, between those terminals that are to be shunted by you. That means the meter will do the same thing as when you touch the two meter wires together when you hit the correct terminals to be shunted. In our example, jumping pins A and B will give you free 110, jumping pins C and D will give free 220. Pin E is ground, and don't jump that to anything. When installing jumper wires, strip off the insulation 2" from the end and wrap it around the prong as shown. The wire must be wrapped around the part of the prong near the plastic base of the meter or it won't fit back into the sockets in the meter pan. Be sure the bare part of the wire touches only the proper prongs and stays clear of all others.

Now, carefully fit the prongs into the sockets and firmly push the meter into the pan. It may not go flush, but push it in and put the ring over the meter and screw it shut. Forget the lock if you removed one.

What will happen now is that the shunt will bypass some of the electricity around your meter, but not all. The thin-ner wires (#16) will only bypass some of the electricity. The meter will run slower than it normally would. The larger wires (#14 or #12) will stop the meter almost com-pletely. This is a mixed blessing, because it looks suspic-ious and should only be done in fiscal emergencies. We'll let you know better and easier ways to bypass meters as soon as we hear from you about them.

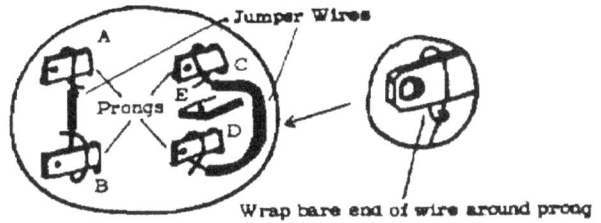

Wrap bare end of wire around prong

RESTORING POWER

Two ways of commonly cutting off your electricity are removing your meter (Yea!) or by slipping little rubber sleeves over the prongs of the meter, thus preventing the prongs from contacting the sockets.

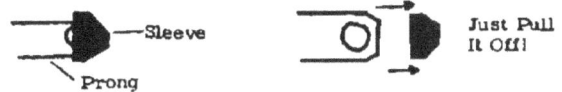

To get around these methods is easy. Just put in another meter, or jump the socket with wires. If you do this, be prepared for a visit from a Electric Co. representative. Be ignorant but nice. "A jumper? What the heck is a jum-per?" Or you can jump the socket from behind the meter pan so that even if the meter is gone they won't see the wires. This will hopefully be explained in a future issue.

To remove the plastic sleeves from the meter prongs is easy, but they'll notice (maybe) that your meter reading is going up and your wheel is moving, so you should install jumpers too. In fact, you can leave on the sleeves and very carefully install the jumpers so the meter is dead but the jumpers are live. That may require some work, though. ANY IDEAS?

Or, you can do the safest trip of all, and that's to steal it from your landlord. Only do this if you hate your land-lord, but of course don't do it anyway. Just tap the wires from a hall light or an outside light and run them into your apartment. The maximum current you can use is then det-

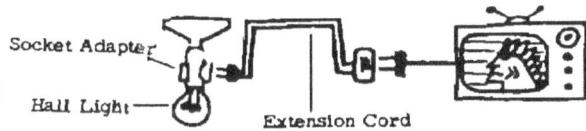

ermined by the fuse of the hall or outside light circuit. If you use too much current, the fuse will blow and you'll have to wait until it's replaced to get electricity from that circuit. When wiring outside, use thick, weatherproof cable.

All power wiring must be done intelligently. Otherwise you can have a fire. So here is how to figure your current demands: Each appliance you use eats up a certain number of watts. 110 volt appliances use 1 amp (or ampere) for every 100 watts of power. 220 volt appliances use 1/2 amp for every 100 watts. You'll usually be using 110 volts, so obtain #16 wire for handling up to 1000 watts, and #14 wire for 1000 watts or more. Hardware stores will have all the plugs and sockets and wire you need with people who can show you how to hook it up.

Hide all "tap" jobs by routing the wires through walls or above ceilings. Camouflaging sometimes helps. If you tap off of a hall light, be sure to replace the bulb each time it blows. If someone else does it they may see your handiwork.

Whenever you do a tap job, pay attention to safety rules. If possible, turn off the circuit while you're working on it. Find the switch or the fuse that turns it off. If you must work on it while it's live, get a friend who knows how. It's dangerous, and one must use insulated tools and have enough dexterity to be able to work with gloves on. We suggest you find the fuse and have someone hold a flashlight. If anyone asks, you're just changing the bulb.

PICKING THE LOCK

To make a key for a rollersmith lock, take a 2" nail, size 8D or slightly larger, and bend up the tip a little as shown. You may have to tap it with a hammer to insert it a full inch and an eighth. Then use the bent tip to hook one of the rings inside. Pull the nail out very slowly and powerfully with a big pliers or visegrips. The spring in the lock is very hard and it will slip out a few times before you get it, but when it does the lock will open up. If you can't get it, just get a hacksaw and cut the ring.

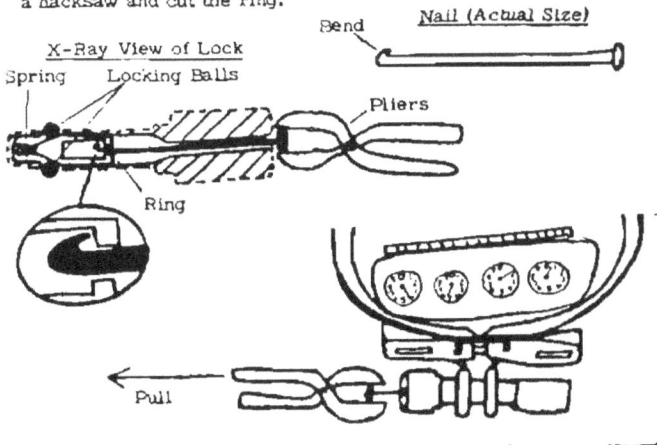

Special thanks to George Metesky's double- DS

Dear TAP,
If anyone there is into short wave and has a receiver that can tune 17,436.5 Kc. (ITT's frequency) for facsimile transmission, you can intercept all sorts of memos, schematics, etc., by hooking it up to a Xerox 400 Telecopier(rents for $50. a month).
-ML, PENNSYLVANIA-

Dear TAP,
Two good books on sabotage: Beasty Business, (computer sabotage) $1.95 British Book Center, Ecotage, (general sabotage), $1.95 Pocket Books. Also try Laissez-Faire Books, 208 Mercer St., N.Y., N.Y.
-D., NY-

RUMOR DEPT.

We've heard that a certain Judge has declared that Phone Phreaks are only practicing "Malicious mischief" and can not be fined. We also heard that he has declared all fines already paid null and void and returned to Phreakee. Has anyone heard this, and if so, would you send us what you can? (Newspaper articles, names of radio stations, etc.)

DEFENSE FUND

Abbie's defense fund is doing very poorly, probably because of a few myths in peoples minds. One is that the new drug law in N.Y. went into effect after he was busted, so the penalties won't be that bad. But the penalty for cocaine dealing in Abbie's case is MINIMUM 15 years before parole. Maximum (and he may get it) is life. They didn't make that penalty any harsher with the new law, because cocaine was already classed with heroin. To a judge, all white powders are just as dangerous. Well, that's one myth, but the other is that supposedly Abbie ripped off the movement. It's not surprising that our peers like to condemn prominent people, but Abbie is, in the minds of us at TAP, different. He did articles for us, gave us ideas(like raising our price to $2 so we'd stop losing money), helped us (by helping to get Captain Crunch in touch with us   ) and contributed financially. He helped us more than any other single person outside of TAP. Without asking for his name on articles, without asking for publicity or thanks, without expecting anything in return. If you dig what we print, thank Abbie. Isn't it refreshing to hear something nice about Abbie from people who know him? If you believe us, please send some money to Abbie Hoffman & Friends Defense Fund, 640 Broadway, N.Y., N.Y. 10012. Don't send cash. Thanks.

HELP IS NEEDED

We need more information on the following topics for upcoming articles in TAP.
Getting Free Gas and Electricity- What types of meters do you have in your area, and can they catch on to you?
Magnets- Have you heard any weird uses for magnets besides on bulletin boards?
Locks- Code books, picking, drilling, tampering, etc.
Vending Machines- Anything!
Overseas Phone Phreaking- From or to overseas places.
Chemistry- Use your imagination.
Automatic Blue Boxes- Can you believe no one's sent it?

Dear TAP,
I am enclosing this little thought; though I am sure that no one would ever use it for illegal purposes, it is an interesting theory. In many of the older electric co. installations I am told that the wheel they used was of a ferrous alloy, and I have heard of people who, at peak electrical periods (in evenings) attached a small but powerful magnet to either the top or the sides of the electrical meter and actually slowed the meter down so that they were in effect recieving free electricity. Unfortunately the newer meters have aluminum wheels, however the motors which turn them must still be affected by magnetism (and could possibly be slowed?).

Dear TAP,
The part in your article that reads "Women are especially urged to take the course as they usually have a fear of electrical concepts..." should read something like "as they usually have been strongly discouraged from learning electrical concepts." The problem is not women's timidity, but sex-role stereotyping. But it's good you mentioned women in particular.
-S., D.C.-
Note: We should also mention that people of both sexes are strongly discouraged from learning electronics so as to keep us technologically naive and sell us more expensive garbage. Also, of course, to prevent us from tampering with the system. And to keep people on different levels. Course B, Alternating Current is ready. The correspondence courses are 50¢ per course (free if you can't afford it). We think that after reading 6 of the courses you should be able to build any project that we've published. We're trying to make it a simple and fast way to learn to build electronics. The first course is Basic Electricity Course A.

Published for informational purposes only by the Technological American Party.

RENEW if your address has a 13 or less next to it.

TAP, ROOM 504, 152 W. 42 ST., N.Y., N.Y. 10036

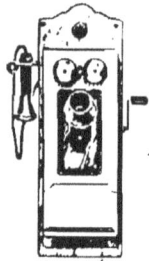